WITHDRAWN
UTSA Libraries

Are New Towns For Lower Income Americans Too?

edited by
**John C. DeBoer
Alexander Greendale**

The Praeger Special Studies program—utilizing the most modern and efficient book production techniques and a selective worldwide distribution network—makes available to the academic, government, and business communities significant, timely research in U.S. and international economic, social, and political development.

Are New Towns For Lower Income Americans Too?

PRAEGER SPECIAL STUDIES IN U.S. ECONOMIC, SOCIAL, AND POLITICAL ISSUES

Praeger Publishers   New York   Washington   London

Library of Congress Cataloging in Publication Data

Main entry under title:

Are new towns for lower-income Americans too?

(Praeger special studies in U.S. economic, social, and political issues)
Based on a conference held at the Institute of Human Relations of the American Jewish Committee, May 31, 1973, sponsored by the Interreligious New Communities Coalition and the National Job-linked Housing Center.
    1. New towns—United States—Congresses. 2. Poor—United States—Congresses. I. DeBoer, John C., ed. II. Greendale, Alexander, ed.
HT167.A82   309.2'62'0973   73-19444
ISBN 0-275-09230-5
ISBN 0-275-63440-X (pbk.)

PRAEGER PUBLISHERS
111 Fourth Avenue, New York, N.Y. 10003, U.S.A.
5, Cromwell Place, London SW7 2JL, England

Published in the United States of America in 1974
by Praeger Publishers, Inc.

All rights reserved

© 1974 by Praeger Publishers, Inc.

Printed in the United States of America

PREFACE

In the 27 years between the time these words are being written and the year 2000, the population of the United States will have increased by some 75 million. That's a lot of people—more than all the people living west of the Mississippi in 1970.

These new millions will require as much more housing, therefore, as existed for all the people west of the Mississippi in 1970, and even more new housing will be required for the additional millions who will join the net migration from the country and small towns to metropolitan areas.* Thus it is estimated that our nation will need to provide new housing for 3 million persons each year for the next 30 years: this is the equivalent of 30 cities the size of Trenton, New Jersey, each year.

For the most part, new homes have been provided by private builders who bought up land; built houses, apartments, cooperatives, or condominiums; and sold or rented them to the public. The result has been the unplanned, erratic, terribly inefficient, land development known as urban sprawl. New homes increase the traffic flow, necessitating the widening of existing roads and the accompanying loss of irreplaceable trees. Many a four-lane highway has been routed, as if in afterthought, through a suburban area, separating homes from schools and merchants from their customers. Desirable but expensive tracts of land near central cities are often leapfrogged by builders in favor of cheaper land further out, widening the sprawl and leaving pockets of unused land.

In the 1960s, however, with the example of the new towns that had been built in Europe, American builders and financiers began to examine an alternate method of increasing the housing supply, by buying a large tract of cheap, undeveloped land outside any metropolitan area and building a planned new city. The developer would start with open fields and build a new city with as many as several hundred thousand residents, complete with the entire infrastructure of a large city, including a central business district, hospitals, schools, etc. Since the developer could plan from the ground up, he could plan streets and walkways that would permit the residents to walk to the schools, neighborhood stores, and other facilities without having to cross a street.

---

*In 1890 only 35 percent of the U.S. population lived in urban areas and 65 percent in the country, but 73 percent lived in urban areas and only 27 percent in the country by 1970.

If the developer could solve the gigantic problems of financing such a project, he could create a very desirable new community as an alternative to urban sprawl—and make money in the process. In actual fact, those who were among the early residents in the new town of Columbia, Maryland, have witnessed a phenomenal growth in the value of their homes, and the developer can also realize a considerable profit on the continuing sale of the land, which he bought quite reasonably before anyone was aware that it was to become part of a new city.

The new town idea seems to be one whose time has come, and many new towns have been born since 1960. Although none of them has yet grown to full size, about 200,000 persons have moved into them. Millions more are yet to be accommodated in the scores of new, planned cities that are still only gleams in the eyes of their developers. Up to half of the new dwelling units built in this country at the end of the century will be in these new towns.

So far the new towns in America, unlike those in Britain and Japan, have largely benefited the affluent. For example, the median family income in Columbia, Maryland, is over $15,000. But a number of groups are determined to make the new towns in America a breakthrough for everyone and not just for those of higher income. Such groups believe that America should have an urban growth policy that will permit the man who sweeps out the shopping mall in the new town to live in the new town along with those who shop there. He, too, should be able to afford the amenities the new communities provide, and his children should be able to enjoy a park outside the back door instead of being sequestered in a decaying urban ghetto; at the present time few such persons can afford to live in new communities. Further, semiskilled and unskilled jobs should also be planned for these new communities in order to insure that lower income Americans will be included in the new towns movement.

New towns are increasingly becoming part of the federal agenda. The Department of Housing and Urban Development (HUD) has been authorized under Title VII of the Housing and Urban Development Act of 1970 to make loan guarantees of up to $50 million to new town developers, public or private. The government does not lend the money: it guarantees the loans (for a fee), and it puts strings on the developers. In order to qualify, developers must plan their new towns to house both low and high income persons in a mix that resembles a cross section of the population in the area. They must also build with respect for the environment and otherwise conform to federal guidelines. HUD expects to approve ten new towns a year for such loan guarantees.

One of the groups concerned with housing for low and moderate income people provided within new towns is the Interreligious New

Communities Coalition (INCC), and another is the National Job-Linked-Housing Center (NJLHC). These two groups joined in sponsoring a national consultation in New York City on May 31, 1973, the theme of which was the same as the title of this book. The papers presented then, along with the discussions they prompted, form the contents of this book.

The cosponsors represent religious and human-relations institutions to whom new towns are a hope for a better life for all Americans. Many of those who attended the conference were government representatives, labor officials, builder-developers, corporation executives, architects, and planners, who are interested in new towns for much the same reasons: they see new towns not only as profit-making ventures but also as new communities that can provide some curative remedies for our urban problems, while at the same time creating more democratic living arrangements than are currently available.

The consultation had two purposes: (1) to bring together a number of people representing new town builder-developers; corporate officials; planners; architects; and legislative, religious, and human-relations leaders, as well as others who have an interest in including lower income Americans in new towns; and (2) to provide an opportunity for groups representing lower income Americans to become acquainted and to decide whether the time was propitious for the formation of a network or coalition for furthering this common interest.

The format for the day was as follows: the morning and luncheon speakers addressed themselves to the conference theme, defined in their own terms the phrase "lower income Americans," and accepted questions from the floor. After lunch the panel reactors commented on the morning proceedings, and then the conference participants broke up into small groups to explore the question, "Is there a need for a network of organizations that address the issue of the needs of lower income Americans in new towns?"

Those invited to speak at the morning session had expertise in various facets of the conference theme. Edward Lamont is the director of the Office of New Community Development in HUD. Floyd McKissick is the developer of a new town, Soul City, designed particularly with lower income Americans in mind. D. David Brandon is the Director of Program Development of the Urban Development Corporation of New York State (UDC), the only such public development corporation in this country. Hugh Mields is one of the most sought-after new town consultants in the country and has written widely on the subject. Bernard Weissbourd is a new town builder-developer and a creative thinker in the new town field, whose articles on satellite cities have attracted national attention. Gus Tyler, Assistant

Vice President of the ILGWU, is highly regarded as a creative and innovative lecturer and writer.

The liveliest part of the consultation was the after-luncheon discussion of the papers given in the morning, sparked by a panel of responders representing groups that speak for lower income Americans of various kinds, such as blacks, Hispanic Americans, and tenants, and also by a noted new town builder who represented the League of New Community Developers.

The consultation did bring to the surface a desire on the part of a number of participants to form a loose, informal network that would be a clearinghouse of information and a consortium for joint action of various kinds. This would include efforts to put new towns for lower income Americans on the national public agenda. Hopefully, governmental input into new towns may also stimulate business and industry to provide the jobs necessary to make new towns viable communities for those of low and moderate income. It is the intention of the sponsors of this conference to promote this in the immediate years ahead.

John C. DeBoer
Alexander Greendale

CONTENTS

		Page
PREFACE		v
CONFERENCE COSPONSORS		xi
CONFERENCE PARTICIPANTS		xii

Chapter

1	HUMAN CONCERNS IN THE PUBLIC DEVELOPMENT CORPORATION D. David Brandon	1
2	HUD AND NEW TOWNS Edward Lamont	9
3	THE FREE-STANDING NEW TOWN: NEW OPTIONS? Floyd B. McKissick	19
4	LEGISLATIVE FRONTIERS: LOWER INCOME AMERICANS AND NEW TOWNS Hugh Mields, Jr.	31
5	SATELLITE COMMUNITIES: TOWARD A RATIONAL GROWTH POLICY Bernard Weissbourd	44
6	THE IMPACT OF JOB-LINKED-HOUSING ON LABOR AND NEW COMMUNITIES Gus Tyler	51
7	RESPONSE PANEL Glenn Claytor, Maria Perez, Cushing N. Dolbeare, Robert E. Simon, Jr.	56

Chapter		Page
8	PLENARY SESSION	68
ABOUT THE EDITORS		77

CONFERENCE COSPONSORS

The Interreligious New Communities Coalition (INCC) was organized in 1972 as a voluntary membership organization consisting of the officially designated representatives of a dozen Protestant denominations, The U.S. Catholic Conference, and the American Jewish Committee. The Protestant denominations are the American Baptist Convention, the American Lutheran Church, the Christian Church/ Disciples of Christ, the Lutheran Church in America, the Lutheran Church Missouri Synod, the Lutheran Council in the U.S.A., the Presbyterian Church in the U.S., the Reformed Church in America, the Southern Baptist Convention, the United Church of Christ, the United Methodist Church, and the United Presbyterian Church.

Administratively, INCC is related to the Joint Strategy and Action Committee (JSAC), a consortium of national mission agencies of the above and other Protestant denominations. INCC has a twofold purpose: (1) planning for the presence of organized religion in new towns, and (2) influencing the planned social structures of new towns, that they may be places where all God's children, and whatever race or class, may find the abundant life together.

The National Job-Linked-Housing Center (NJLHC) is a program of the Institute of Human Relations of the American Jewish Committee (AJC). Basic to AJC philosophy is the belief that the denial of justice or equal opportunity to any religious, racial, or ethnic group constitutes a threat to the rights of all. The NJLHC is committed to developing strategies and programs that increase the housing supply of low-skilled and semiskilled working Americans, and that reduce the polarization of society, which is now escalating because of the dearth of adequate housing for these workers. The new towns have the potential for providing housing, jobs, and positive intergroup relationships for a broad spectrum of Americans, and are thus high on the Center's programmatic and "human relations" agenda.

CONFERENCE PARTICIPANTS

Speakers

D. DAVID BRANDON was appointed Director of Program Development for the New York State Urban Development Corporation in February 1971. He is responsible for UDC's long-range planning for urban development needs throughout the state. Mr. Brandon has held executive positions on several county planning boards and related professional groups in the field of urban development.

EDWARD LAMONT is Director of the Office of New Communities Development, Department of Housing and Urban Development. For ten years prior to joining HUD, Mr. Lamont was with Morgan Guaranty Trust Company of New York. He was also a director of the State Street Investment Corporation of Boston. Between 1951 and 1961 he was employed in Washington, D.C. by the Mutual Security Agency, the International Bank of Reconstruction and Development (World Bank), and the International Finance Corporation, a World Bank subsidiary.

FLOYD B. McKISSICK is the developer of the new town of Soul City, in North Carolina. In 1966 Mr. McKissick was appointed National Director of the Congress of Racial Equality, and his active stewardship of CORE is well known. He currently heads Floyd B. McKissick Enterprises, Inc., a national security company formed to help organize and finance black businesses across the nation. He is also President of Warren Regional Planning Corporation, Inc., the technical planning arm of McKissick Enterprises.

HUGH MIELDS, Jr. is Vice-President of the Washington D.C. law firm of Linton, Mields, and Costen, Inc. He is currently serving as a consultant on urban programs to the mayor of Chicago; as Washington representative for the city of Norfolk; as legislative consultant to the League of New Community Developers; and as an advisor to the Redevelopment Land Agency of the District of Columbia and the Newfields new town in Ohio.

BERNARD WEISSBOURD presently serves on the boards of directors of the Metropolitan Planning and Housing Council, and the Center for the Study of Democratic Institutions; the advisory council of the Northeastern Planning Commission; and the New Communities Council of the Urban Land Institute. In 1959 Mr. Weissbourd formed Metropolitan Structures, Inc., which is currently engaged in the creation of two pioneering "new-towns-in-town," one in Montreal, Canada, and the other in downtown Chicago.

GUS TYLER is Assistant President of the International Ladies' Garment Workers Union. He directs the ILGWU Departments of Education, Politics, and Training, and administers the ILGWU National Scholarship Fund and the David Dubinsky Foundation. He sits on numerous research, legal, and social policy boards as chairman, director, and member. Mr. Tyler is the Editor of <u>Politeia</u>, a publication of the American Association of Political Consultants.

Response Panel

GLENN CLAYTOR is a member of the boards of directors of the Non-Profit Housing Center, the National Housing Conference, Inc., and the Housing Assistance Council, Inc. In 1969 he was appointed Director of Housing for the National Urban League.

MARIA PEREZ is the Regional Director of the National Spanish-Speaking Housing Development Corporation. She is a board member of the Health Insurance Plan of Greater New York, the Senior Citizen Committee of the Community Council of Greater New York, and the Lower East Side Community Corporation.

CUSHING N. DOLBEARE is Consultant on Housing Policy for the National Tenants Organization. She has served as Managing Director of the Housing Association of Delaware Valley, and Assistant Director of the Philadelphia Housing Association.

ROBERT E. SIMON, Jr. is currently serving as Chairman of the Board of Riverton Properties, Inc., which is developing a 2,500-acre new town in New York State. His company, Simon Enterprises, Inc., owns and manages commercial and residential properties in the United States and Canada. Mr. Simon represented the League of New Community Developers at the conference.

Question and Answer Participants

Rev. Raymond Brown, Board of Church Extension, Indianapolis, Ind.
David Burton, Builder-Developer
William Chambers, United Presbyterian Church, New York, N.Y.

Rev. William Deutschman, American Lutheran Church, Columbia, Md.
John J. Edwards, Jr., Director of Planning, Suburban Action Institute, Tarrytown, N.Y.
Rev. Albert Erickson, Lutheran Housing Coalition, Fargo, N.D.
Rev. Howell Foster, Jr., Lutheran Council, Huntington Beach, Calif.
Samuel Freedman, Director, Division of Business and Industry, American Jewish Committee, New York, N.Y.
Rev. John Hager, United Methodist Church, New York, N.Y.
Rev. James Hamblen, Southern Baptist Convention, Columbia, Md.
Richard Hansen, Tri-State Regional Planning Commission, New York, N.Y.
Rev. Lonnie Hass, Director, Church Establishment of the Christian Church, Indianapolis, Ind.
Edward Holmgren, National Committee Against Discrimination in Housing, Washington, D.C.
Rev. Robert Johnson, Interreligious Coalition for Housing, New York, N.Y.
Rev. Donald Larsen, Lutheran Council U.S.A., New York, N.Y.
Robert Litke, Welfare Island Development Corp., New York, N.Y.
Rev. Glenn Orr, American Baptist Board of National Ministries, Valley Forge, Pa.
Al Pierce, Exploratory Project for Economic Alternatives, Cambridge, Mass.
Carl Sussman, Cambridge Policy Studies Institute, Cambridge, Mass.
Peggy Wireman, Department of Housing and Urban Development, Washington, D.C.

Are New Towns For Lower Income Americans Too?

CHAPTER 1

**HUMAN CONCERNS IN
THE PUBLIC DEVELOPMENT
CORPORATION**
D. David Brandon

The Urban Development Corporation has been trying to carry out a balanced program in New York State. Edward J. Logue, President of UDC, feels that the problems of low income and poor housing cannot be solved in the city alone, but must be viewed in the context of the total urban structure, including the suburbs and surrounding area. Therefore, UDC has tried to develop housing where the jobs are, and today they are often in the suburbs. New suburban factories require housing at a reasonable cost nearby for their employees.

This on-going program has worked well around the state. The stumbling block was UDC's attempt to carry out this type of program in Westchester County, at the invitation of county government. The need was well documented in various planning surveys and studies undertaken in recent years; over 60,000 new jobs have been created since 1960, and about 80 percent of those who work in the county earn less than $12,000 per year. Even schoolteachers, firemen, and policemen often cannot live in the towns they serve because of the cost of housing.

UDC felt that a modest beginning would be a fair-share program of 100 housing units in each of nine towns, but this became an inflammatory issue that placed the state legislature under great pressure. The resulting action of the state legislature will affect UDC activities, but should not completely defeat the suburban effort. The new legislation provides a town or village with a veto over each housing proposal during the 30 days following UDC's project public hearing. In the past the UDC Board of Directors had the responsibility of weighing the public hearing results and modifying or dropping the proposal based upon their judgment of the broader public interest.

The change means that cooperation between UDC, the town or village, and supporting citizens will need to be much stronger to assure that reactionary groups opposed to low and moderate income housing cannot frighten the municipality into a veto. In most places in the state UDC has been invited in, and the change in the law should not particularly affect those areas.

Turning to the subject of the day, there is no question in the minds of us at UDC that new towns are for lower income Americans, too. Our ability to carry out that promise is less limited than it is for many other agencies. In recent years Americans have become aware of the unique opportunity of new communities to provide a better-planned physical environment and community relationship. Random development of housing, businesses, and other enterprises has generally failed on both these counts.

The history of planned settlements goes back through many centuries, but the revival of them here in the United States during the last decade bodes well for our country's third century. The new community attempts to assure the optimum social, physical, and economic environment for its residents. More precisely, efforts in recent years have focused on the development of balanced communities that take into account the various income and age levels, as well as individual preferences for housing types and life styles. The challenge of creating a balanced and open community of this type is a great one and is only partly being met by the new communities now under construction.

Recent federal interest in new communities solidified in the late 1960s with the development of a program to assist private enterprise in undertaking comprehensive new community projects. Through a system of debt guarantee, private enterprise was encouraged to enter into projects that are more comprehensive and require larger investment committments with longer construction buildout periods. In 1970 modification of this federal program made it possible for governmental bodies, as well as private enterprise, to participate in this process.

In New York State, interest in comprehensively dealing with human problems and environments has existed for some time, and a number of specific actions have resulted from this interest including the creation of the New York State Urban Development Corporation in 1968. This public benefit corporation was granted the power to deal comprehensively with various community development matters and was given a social and public purpose mandate. In its role as a state agency that works closely with private enterprise, government officials, and local citizens, it develops and finances housing for low, moderate, and middle income families; assists industrial and commercial development as a means of creating and expanding job opportunities; redevelops and upgrades blighted and deteriorating areas to provide land improvement; and undertakes construction of educational, cultural, and other civic facilities to assure full opportunity for delivery of various social and governmental services.

At the same time, the State Planning Office was attempting to bring to the state administration and its agencies a sense of comprehensiveness and goal-oriented programming. Many of the state agencies have now established planning officers as key members of their leadership teams. Agency budgets and programs are reflecting this interest, and various social, economic, and physical planning programs and organizational relationships are assisting in the evolution of an open and effective process.

Out of this effort came a special study of new communities jointly undertaken by the State Office of Planning Coordination and the Urban Development Corporation. In a report entitled "New Communities for New York," a proposal was made for using new communities as a means of structuring growth and development over the next 30 years and assuring a healthy and attractive environment for a broad range of people, rich and poor, skilled and unskilled, black and white.

The Urban Development Corporation has served to carry forward this proposal through the establishment of three new communities within the state. These are located on Welfare Island* in New York City, in the town of Lysander to the northwest of Syracuse, and in the town of Amherst to the northeast of Buffalo.

The first of these, Welfare Island, is a new-town-in-town, which will create an optimum community environment in the midst of our nation's largest city. Over 2,000 of the 5,000 dwelling units planned are currently under construction, with the first occupancy scheduled for 1974. This new community of approximately 18,000 people will be completed by the end of this decade.

Welfare Island is designed to assure an economically and ethnically integrated community. Of the dwelling units, 1,500 are designed for persons and families who have low income, and 500 of these are designed and reserved for those who are elderly. Moderate income families will occupy 1,250 units, and 1,000 are designed for the use of those with middle income. A final 1,250 dwelling units will be available to those who have middle-upper and upper incomes.

The development program for the island is unique in many ways. Physically, the community will be grouped in two villages with a common town center. The two large existing hospitals, Bird S. Coler and Goldwater, employ approximately 4,200 people and will continue to function on the island and to provide service to the new community. An effort is being made to provide housing for individuals requiring only outpatient care, as well as housing for employees.

---

*The island's name was recently changed to Roosevelt Island.

An important aspect of the new community will be a system of public school spaces immediately adjacent to the apartment buildings. This system takes advantage of the opportunity to start from scratch and will enable the development and incorporation of the best approaches in modern education; this effort is being carried out in partnership with the New York City Board of Education.

Private automobiles are being eliminated from the island and will stop at a large parking terminal known as Motorgate. A free mini-transit system of electric buses will be available throughout the island. An aerial tramway will link the island directly with Manhattan, as will a subway line, which is currently under construction and will be opened in 1980.

An underground pneumatic refuse collection system will eliminate the need for garbage trucks on the island and will provide improved environmental conditions while at the same time reducing costs to the city for sanitation service.

The new community will contain many active urban areas, but nearly one-third of its total of 147 acres will be used for parks. An ecological park is planned near the Coler Hospital at the northern end of the island. There will also be smaller sitting parks and an active sports park. A promenade is being constructed that will surround the entire island and will also make it accessible from the water.

A series of objectives serves as a basis for the development of this new community and is as follows:

1. To develop an economic and racially balanced community
2. To provide residents with a wide range of services and amenities
3. To ban private automobiles from the community circulation system
4. To develop innovative methods for delivery of social services including health care, geriatric care, legal services, and family support services
5. To develop a tranquil yet urban environment
6. To maximize spatial amenities for the residents
7. To serve as a model for similar developments elsewhere
8. To restore significant historical landmarks and functionally integrate these structures into the life of the community
9. To create a controlled complexity in the physical environment, while retaining human scale
10. To assure accessible and usable open space
11. To preserve and enhance the natural environment of the area.

The two upstate communities under development by the Urban Development Corporation are based upon similar goals, although the physical context of these communities is somewhat different. In each case they are located in a suburbanizing section of a large metropolitan area. Because of the greater availability of land under these circumstances, the communities are able to utilize a broad open-space system, with a clustering of neighborhoods and community facilities.

In Lysander, some 2,700 acres will include 5,000 dwelling units housing approximately 18,000 people; 30 percent will be for low income, with 10 percent reserved for low income elderly; 20 percent will be for moderate income families; and the remaining 50 percent for middle and upper income.

A large industrial park is being developed to assure adequate job opportunities for all of those residing within the community, as well as for people from the surrounding area. Commercial, social, recreational, educational, and other facilities are being planned as part of a complete community. A special effort is being made to launch a complete health services system, which can serve as a pilot for the larger metropolitan area.

In the new community of Audubon, located near Buffalo in the town of Amherst, there will be approximately 9,000 dwelling units, with a range of styles and economic levels including units for low-income elderly and low income family as well as for moderate, middle, and upper income persons and families. No large industrial base is planned in this instance, since the new community is associated with a major new State University Center campus, which will provide jobs for students, faculty, and staff, and also employment opportunities in related commercial enterprises.

The three new communities now underway demonstrate the interest in human concerns held by the New York State Urban Development Corporation. The partnership between the Corporation and the other public and private participants in these efforts shows that such an approach is viable.

Public development corporations have a unique role to play in joining the best of private initiative and financial capacity with the human and public purposes of government. Public-private new town partnerships offer an opportunity to assure housing and job opportunities for those of all ages and income levels within a context of balanced community and social programs and services.

Discussion

FREEDMAN: Would you be good enough to give us the ranges of the various categories of income in terms of dollars for lower middle, moderate, and low income?

BRANDON: The categories are those used by the federal government because we are tied to federal programs. This raises an interesting question in the year 1973, since the President has placed a moratorium on housing programs since early in January. Both public and private developers now have no means of bringing the actual rental cost or purchase cost of housing down to these levels. There were some exemptions to the Presidential moratorium, including new communities that are under the federal Title VII program. At the moment commitments seem to be in place for these existing new communities, and presumably the moratorium is only temporary. Only time will tell what actually comes about and whether there will continue to be housing programs to assist low and moderate income families as part of new communities.

Let me give you an example of a new neighborhood UDC is building in Niagara Falls, which includes quite a cross section of housing. It is designed with rentals, co-ops, and single family homes for sale. A widow living only on social security could be renting an apartment for as low as $32 a month; the market price on that same apartment would be several times that amount. It takes the commitment of some kind of state or federal program to make that lower rent possible, since the basic costs of construction, interest, maintenance, and management have not changed. The State Urban Development Corporation has some cost advantages, since it has no tax and profit lines.

It is my view that the federal government must continue to be the basis for these housing assistance programs, since no single state has the financial capacity to deal with them. There has to be a national policy and a national program.

CONFEREE: * You listed several categories, low, moderate, and middle income for Welfare Island, with a number of units allocated to each one of these income groups. Are those units separated by building arrangements, or are they income-integrated within each building?

BRANDON: Our basic policy has been to build moderate income housing and then, by using different techniques and financial programs, assure that low income families and individuals can also live in it. For example, a housing complex of a hundred units would usually have 70 percent of its units reserved for moderate income families and individuals. These are usually working people who are holding jobs but who just don't earn enough money to be able to afford adequate housing. The remaining 30 percent of the housing units are reserved for low income, and of those 30 percent UDC normally would reserve 10 percent for the low income elderly.

---

*Several questioners neglected to identify themselves.

Now, on Welfare Island that same general principle holds, although there are some buildings that will be for middle and high income. However, because the new community is designed the way it is, these buildings are side by side and the mixing of all income levels will exist. The island is 800 feet at its widest part, and the housing is grouped in two villages. It's awfully hard to say one section is high income and another is low when they really are all right there, cheek to jowl. It's all one community as far as we're concerned, and to the extent that building finance can be structured, UDC has economically integrated the buildings themselves.

PIERCE: I'm interested in the question of economics for new towns, which also affects the income level of people who can live in them. And I'm interested in the third new town you mentioned in Amherst. First, did the UDC move in on preexisting plans of the university to locate this facility there; and second, does the UDC intend to look at other planned locational or contracting decisions by state government or federal government and capitalize on those for an economic base?

BRANDON: Well, as planners, and I was the New York State Planning Director before I moved to UDC to head the program development division, we do attempt to capture the economic push of such public decisions as those concerning new highways, utility extensions, university centers, employment centers, etc.

In the case of Audubon, throughout the early 1960s there was a continuing debate over whether the university center for western New York should be in the center of Buffalo or in suburbia. That was before I became involved with state activities, but there are consultant studies favoring the center of Buffalo and an equal number of studies that favor the suburbs. In this particular case the decision was made to locate in the suburban town of Amherst.

Because Amherst is one of the more affluent and more rapidly growing suburbs there was a potential problem of housing for faculty, staff, and students at reasonable cost. The state planning office undertook a special corridor study that extended from the center city to the suburban town of Amherst and included various hospitals and other public institutions. Out of the study came proposals for a new mass transit system as well as for housing and other developments.

The governor then came to the town of Amherst for a visit, bringing with him Edward Logue of the Urban Development Corporation and various state planning officials. During that visit he requested the UDC to see that there would be adequate housing and other facilities for the whole range of people who would be associated with the university. The response of the UDC was the development of the new community of Audubon.

EDWARDS: In your new communities, how much consideration have you given to a correlation between anticipated job levels among the resident population that you anticipate in these new communities?

BRANDON: We have not undertaken highly focused studies. On the other hand, we have attempted to see that the basic economic structure of the area is mirrored in what is done in the new community. Using Audubon as an example, an agreement with the town and university officials calls for a housing program that reflects future needs.

In Lysander, depending on the nature of the firms locating in the industrial park, there may be a need to adjust the housing composition. While the State University is reasonably predictable, the numerous private decisions in industrial location are not, and some of the fine tuning for the housing may have to be made during the years of development.

CHAPTER

2

HUD AND NEW TOWNS
Edward Lamont

While our friend David Brandon from UDC is still here I'd like to say that at HUD we are great admirers of the initiative that New York State has taken in establishing a state development corporation to engage in erecting housing for low and moderate income people, and in undertaking the planning and development of new communities. We only wish that other states around the country would go down that same road. One of the strongest objectives in our presently proposed legislation at this time is to provide encouragement to the states to take greater initiative in planning and controlling the use of land, as well as establishing agencies to plan and carry out community development.

I'm going to tell you a little bit about our program and then I'm going to be more specific in citing the role of our new communities program as a setting for housing for low and moderate income families. Housing is not really the appropriate word; the new towns will provide a total living environment for their residents. Of the many challenges facing our society today, I believe that the most critical is to create a new living environment for millions of our citizens.

I'm convinced that the present pattern of population settlement in this country is the main source of some of our most dangerous social, environmental, and economic problems. The pattern is marked by the draining of population from rural areas to a small number of densely congested central cities and by a flight by higher and middle income families and business from inner cities to the suburbs. The residents of the cities and the suburbs are increasingly polarized by income, by race, by quality of education, and by all the other conditions affecting the quality of life. It's a situation that has disastrous portents for the increasingly unmanageable inner city and its suburbs, whose destinies are so closely linked together.

Of course, as Secretary Romney and others have said, the total metropolitan region is in fact one social and economic unit. It is the "real city," and more planning should be done on this regional scale. However, fragmented planning and polarizing trends continue. They are usually characterized by urban sprawl or affluent subdivisions— poorly planned, uncoordinated, piecemeal, small-scale development that often despoils the natural environment. This is an extremely costly means of development. A very promising alternative to these unhealthy trends is well planned, large-scale new community development; this brings us to our program.

Our basic method of assistance is to guarantee the debt of new community land development companies, private or public, up to 50 million dollars per project. The developer may use these funds for land acquisition and development, for installing water and sewer lines and access roads, and for payment of his overhead expenses. The developer prepares the land for eventual sale for residential, commercial, or industrial purposes, all according to a development and land-use plan that has been agreed to by HUD. That guarantee enables him to borrow a substantial amount of money on a long-term basis, with a repayment schedule that fits the project's cash flow. With the government guarantee the interest rate is moderate. Not all of the funds are guaranteed loans; we require the developer to put up a significant amount of his own capital in the form of an equity contribution.

What are the objectives of our program?
1. Redress of the rural-urban imbalance, with free-standing communities or small town additions to serve as economic growth centers and stem the flow of the out-migration that has been taking place from many inland rural areas. The only free-standing town for which we've announced our assistance so far is Soul City. Floyd McKissick is here to give you a full story on that project. But this is the type of town we want very much to assist, and it has a very high priority in the projects we consider.
2. Revitalization of the inner city through new-towns-in-town. David Brandon has already told you about Welfare Island. We have a special program for public bodies such as UDC that can borrow successfully on their own and don't really need our guarantee assistance; we review their plans and make a "determination of eligibility," which means in fact that the new community has met the federal standards under our act and regulations. Both in the case of Welfare Island and Lysander, we have made that finding. This determination enables the new community to receive the same priority as other approved new communities under federal grant or housing-assistance programs. While there may be some question at a given time about the character of such programs

in the future, we are dealing with long-term plans, normally 15 to 20 years in development.

I sincerely believe that federally approved new towns will enjoy the highest priority in whatever programs are developed in the future for housing or other forms of assistance for community development.

3. Control of suburban growth. According to the 1970 census 65 percent of our population lived in metropolitan areas, 36 percent in the suburbs, and only 29 percent in the inner cities. For the first time the suburbs have as many jobs as the inner cities. Polls continue to show that many people prefer to live outside the inner city.

We must bring orderly and rational growth to the suburbs and give more people a choice about where they can live. Many low and moderate income people are locked in inner city slums, unable to follow the movement of jobs to the suburbs. All the new towns we assist contain a substantial portion of housing for people of low and moderate income. We believe that the settlement of low income people in our new towns will take place without the tensions that so often characterize the proposed construction of low income projects in developed suburban areas, since the mixed character and social goals of the new community are well-known and accepted from the beginning.

So far we have announced our assistance of twelve satellite new towns, of two new-towns-in-town, and of Soul City, a free-standing town.

4. Innovation: we believe that new communities provide an excellent laboratory for innovative technological systems of waste disposal and transportation as well as for social programs.

5. Economy: large-scale planning, land acquisition, and development are far less costly than conventional piecemeal uncoordinated growth, which is characterized by rapidly escalating land costs. Thus, new community planning and development fights one of the most virulent forms of inflation in this country.

I would like to briefly describe what we mean by a "new community." This is a phrase that is bandied about with a wide variety of meanings. What do we mean by the term at HUD, as we review the plans of new community sponsors seeking our financial assistance?

A new community must have most if not all of the basic activities and facilities normally associated with a city or town, including a substantial job base. The size must be significant in comparison with the existing development or communities in the area. We have assisted communities that have ranged in potential population from 20,000 to 150,000 people.

The project must be economically feasible in terms of its base and potential for growth, and it must have a sound financial plan. It must have a favorable long-term fiscal impact on the area in which it will be located. Certainly, an important reason for some of the resistance in the suburbs to the suggested construction of low income housing stems from a concern about the fiscal impact. Suburban residents ask, "Will this project require a higher property tax to be paid by existing residents for increased educational and other services?" In all of our new communities we require a fiscal impact study to be made as part of the application process. This is a very important part of our review.

There must be a general planning and development program designed to maintain an attractive environment, including a suitable site, sound land use and transportation plans, sufficient environmental protection measures, adequate public facilities, appropriate architectural review procedures, enough recreational and social facilities, etc. One of the most time-consuming and important parts of our review is the preparation of the environmental impact statement, which is circulated to all interested federal and local agencies for comment.

I have already said that a substantial amount of housing for persons and families of low and moderate income must be built. In determining the adequacy of the housing plan we take into account the income profile for the entire urban area; the housing demand and supply in the market area of the project; and the projected employment and income levels derived therefrom in the new community.

The developer must formulate and implement an affirmative action program for equal opportunity in housing, employment, and business. For example, he would advertise in media that reach minority families regarding the availability of housing and business opportunities in the new town. We urge the developer to have appropriate minority representation on his own staff.

A full range of governmental services must also be provided. The plan for the new community must be consistent with areawide planning. All state and local reviews and approvals that are necessary must of course be obtained.

Finally, we look very carefully into the experience and ability of the developer, be it a private company or public agency, to carry out the very difficult and complex job of planning and developing a new town.

What have we achieved so far in our program? We have announced our assistance to 15 new communities, which at peak population, say in 15 years, will accommodate 870,000 people. The total amount of U.S. guarantee authority we have committed comes to $293 million. If 10 projects were approved annually for 10 years, some 100 new communities would be initiated, and based on existing sizes, they would encompass some 570,000 acres and serve a peak population at full development of 5.8 million people. A total of 6.7 million people would be served, including the new communities already approved.

There are 280,000 projected housing units in the 15 approved new communities, and the developers have agreed to provide 28 percent of this number of housing units for persons of low and moderate income, of which approximately 10 percent will be for families of low income.

One of our key goals in new communities is to permit people to live and work in the same community, reducing the need for costly highways and time-consuming and fatiguing trips to work. In our 15 new communities there are plans to provide about 227,000 jobs. Thus, 85 percent of the heads of households can work in the new towns if they so choose. We recognize, of course, that some people who live in new towns work elsewhere and vice versa. But the creation of a diversified job base, with jobs representing a whole range of skills and income levels, is extremely important to us. Housing in the community will be related in price to the estimated incomes to be derived from that job base.

Most importantly, new communities should provide a total living environment for everyone, including the low and moderate income people with whom we are especially concerned here today. This includes jobs, housing, recreation, culture, shopping, education, health, transportation, and all of the other facilities and services of a city.

Concern for the physical and natural environment alone is not enough to make a successful new community. Of critical concern too are the needs to be met by the social programs that are planned. I have talked about the housing mix and affirmative action programs intended to bring about equal opportunity in housing and business; we are also emphasizing planning to provide first-rate educational, health, cultural, manpower-training, counselling, and other social service systems in new communities.

Unlike most urban, suburban, and other developments, new communities are planned carefully in advance, with facilities built before each wave of population arrives. Thus, they are among the few locations where communities can avoid future environmental problems, rather than try to play "catch-up" by installing facilities after environmental damage has been incurred. Since the land is under single ownership, density trade-offs permit the owners to maintain large open areas, including flood-plains, woodlands, vistas, and other features that should be preserved from an environmental viewpoint.

There are 20,000 acres of open space designated in the 15 new communities; this represents 23 acres per 1,000 persons at peak development, well above normal standards for neighborhood and citywide open space. Yet the net residential density of the new communities is considerably higher than that of normal suburban development: 24 persons projected per residential acre, compared to approximately 5 to 15 for normal suburban development.

In summary, I think the new communities we are assisting under the federal program will provide a fine living environment for millions of our citizens; they should also serve to set new standards for general community development in the United States.

I'd like now to talk about the role of new communities in providing a setting for people of low and moderate income. Our program is unique as a federal program that by statute and administrative regulation requires provision of substantial amounts of housing for persons and families of low and moderate income in a well-planned total community environment, as a condition of federal project assistance. According to the development plans for the 15 approved new communities, some 77,000 dwelling units will be created for families and persons of low and moderate income by the end of the development period. This amounts to some 28 percent of the total dwelling units in these new communities. That's an average percentage; the new communities vary considerably in proportion because of their different locations.

How do we see that this goal is achieved? In the project agreement with HUD the developers are contractually obligated to develop land, apply for housing subsidies, and use their best efforts to sell low and moderate income housing according to the housing mix plan, subject to annual changes, throughout the 20-year life of a project. We monitor the developer's performance carefully; if he does not live up to his commitments in this respect and does not persuade us that there are justifiable reasons why he is not doing so, we have the power to find him in performance default. We think it is extremely important that our program is designed to deliver a substantial number of low and moderate income housing units in good suburban locations with a minimum of the opposition so often seen in the past.

Secondly, I'd like once again to discuss the creation of a job base, because this is a critical part of our new community plans.

It is vital to have a full range of jobs, going hand in hand with the availability of a substantial amount of housing for people of low and moderate income. It is important to enable people to live close to their work. Industry and commerce will also provide a substantial tax base to help pay for the educational and other services required by the community. Our program, again, is unique in that it delivers such housing in a total, high-quality living environment with amenities in place: schools, shops, parks, social service delivery systems, and employment within easy access. As you know, much of the planning, at least at the neighborhood level, is done on a walking scale. We believe that this program has a great potential for achieving both economic and racial integration on a large-community scale and on a neighborhood scale within these new communities. Our experience is limited, but if we are successful in integrating these new communities, that example will surely not be lost on the populations of existing towns and cities.

Another important aspect of new communities is that they offer an opportunity to test and examine innovative techniques of housing and providing services to persons and families of low and moderate income. Among the items under study right now are direct housing allowances, which could be tested and monitored in new community projects; innovative educational programs and facilities; manpower training programs; methods of housing and providing facilities for the elderly and handicapped; counseling and other social service delivery systems for low income people, health care, and child care.

Why is the new community such a good laboratory for testing innovative technological or social systems that appear to be feasible? Simply because they start off with a clean slate, without the physical or institutional restraints on installing new systems that are found in an existing town or city. They also start with a single developer who has planning control and with the presence of HUD, which is monitoring the development of the new community and urging the developer to use some of these innovative systems.

In summary, new communities embrace all the activities associated with a town. Those built within existing cities can revitalize a blighted area and help curb the flight of business and residents to the suburbs. Others built in rural regions can become economic growth centers and stem the flow of out-migration. Still others will bring orderly and rational growth to the suburbs and provide a fresh opportunity for decent housing and jobs to low and moderate income families now often locked in inner city slums. I believe that as our population grows these new communities can substantially improve the quality of life for millions of our citizens.

Discussion

BURTON: What current efforts are being made by HUD to involve other federal agencies in the new town movement?

LAMONT: We are establishing cooperation agreements with several federal agencies. We already have excellent working arrangements with DOT, HEW, and the National Endowment on The Arts. I'm also hopeful that the federal regional councils, which as you know are located in the ten designated federal regions and include representatives from different government departments, will provide a medium through which the cooperation of all the departments represented on these councils is obtained, for example, on a new community project in that area. Interagency cooperation, I agree, is an extremely important thing, especially in the case of DOT because of the suburban location for many of these new communities; the provision of mass transit systems between them and the central city, which you see so often in the European new towns, is something that is very desirable.

HOLMGREN: You made reference to three towns, I believe, which have resident populations as of this moment, out of 15 which are being supported by the HUD new communities legislation. Could you tell us more specifically about the level of economic and racial integration that does exist in these three towns in terms of achievement and the goals projected.

LAMONT: The three new towns I had in mind were Park Forest South, 30 miles south of the Loop in Chicago; Jonathan, 25 miles from the center of Minneapolis; and Cedar-Riverside, in the heart of Minneapolis and wrapped around the University of Minnesota. Some 1,300 units have been built and occupied in Park Forest South, of which 698 are single family and 591 multifamily. Black occupancy in Park Forest South runs from 6 percent in the condominiums to 28 percent in the single family units; this is the most successfully integrated large-scale development in the Chicago area. However, there have been delays in meeting low and moderate income housing commitments because of environmental disputes over the location of the first low and moderate income development.

In Cedar-Riverside some 1,299 units in a high-rise complex have been completed, but not all are ready for occupancy. Some 424 units have already been rented, of which 239 have been rented to low and moderate income residents: 13 percent of the renters are minority families. Of the 1,299 units, 117 are designated for families of low income (public housing level), 552 for moderate income (section 236 level), and 408 for middle income (state tax reduction, but no federal subsidy), and 222 for market rate. This will be the first project of its kind in the United States with such a mix in the same building complex; this is aimed directly at eliminating the socially stigmatizing practice of forcing low income persons to live in an isolated setting.

Jonathan, located some 25 miles southwest of Minneapolis, has a current population of 1,691 persons and provides 1,021 jobs. It has 524 occupied dwelling units, of which 130 are for persons in the lowest income quartile and 116 for those in the second quartile.

Although occupancy has lagged behind construction, the recent increase in jobs in Jonathan should place this once again in balance. There are 36 minority persons living in Jonathan, or 2.7 percent of the population, which is roughly comparable to the metropolitan minority profile.

CHAMBERS: You said that of the ones that have been approved about 28 percent are below market. Does that represent a balance from a longterm standpoint for the community? Will the developers be able to market those units?

LAMONT: Well, as I indicated, the figure for each project is derived from looking at the income profile for the area; looking at the employment income projections within the project; and looking very practically at the demand and supply for housing at different income levels. Of course, since we're talking about a 15- to 20-year development plan, we recognize that population and market characteristics can change, and so it's to be expected that the appropriate housing mix will change. We sit down each year with the developer and go over the housing mix plan to determine whatever changes appear warranted for the coming year.

PEREZ: I expect that, together with planning, some criteria are established for the measurement of their success. I would like, if possible, to know how you are going to measure the integration of the different families and the minorities. How are they going to be involved, and how are you going to measure this?

LAMONT: Let's talk first about the participation of minorities. I've indicated to you that this is one of the key objectives of our program. Participation is encouraged in various ways: in housing; by the use by developers of minority consultants to assist them in their planning; by the use of minority firms and labor by the contractors and subcontractors working on the project; and by the attraction and development of minority enterprises within the new community. On all of these fronts we use our influence to see that good progress is made. We measure this progress by observation over a period of time and comparison with available regional statistics.

LITKE: This is just a statistical question to put your new town projects in some sort of a context. What percentage of total housing growth up to the year 2000 do you estimate that HUD new towns would account for?

LAMONT: First of all, the towns that we have approved already will accommodate about .9 million people. That would be, say, the

15th year. Now, let us assume we approve ten new towns per year; the average peak population so far has been running about 60,000 people per town, or about 600,000 people a year. In 10 years there would be planned housing for about 6 million people.

These, of course, are rough assumptions; for example, I think that the size of the towns we assist may increase. By the year 2000 we are talking about housing some 13 million people in new communities. You may make your own estimate of population growth in this country; many of the figures seem to cluster around an increase of 65 million by the year 2000. You might say that new communities could conceivably accommodate 20 to 25 percent of population growth by the year 2000.

CHAPTER

3

**THE FREE-STANDING
NEW TOWN:
NEW OPTIONS?**
Floyd B. McKissick

In order to really understand free-standing new communities, and why Soul City in particular is being created, one must bear in mind that the developer of this new town is working from ideas and assumptions that go back to 1968 but remain applicable today. I believe that the struggle for integration in the 1960s must be continued in the 1970s. I think America has been sidetracked, because somehow or other we have not been able to shift gears and recognize what the problems in American society are, and consequently we have not developed strategies for dealing with these problems. In the planning stages for a new community, therefore, we started with an analysis of what actually was happening in America.

What was the battle of the 1960s? We recalled the fight through education and the fight through public accommodations. We remembered the freedom rides and the thrust to bring about integrated public accommodations. We saw many changes occur in the 1960s. And we decided that, in order to make inroads into the degree of racism that existed in American society, new strategies would have to be developed. The 1960s required demonstrations and organization of people—the churches played a role in that organization—and to open doors then we probably required more courage and dedication and commitment on the part of people than are required now. But once we opened these doors, the problem became, how can we go in through the doors? We integrated and, let us say, we penetrated every area in American society—save one. That last barrier is economic integration. We have not yet penetrated it, and we must penetrate it.

When we look at the question, "Are New Towns for Lower Income Americans Too?" we must bear in mind that we can't separate the issue of housing from the greater issues confronting American society. As we look at American society, we see the American city in decay.

I don't know if even Jesus Christ and his disciples could come to New York and solve its problems. I have serious doubts.

In the late 1960s we looked at the cities and we saw welfare; we saw crime in the streets; we saw poor and inadequate housing; we saw discrimination, a lack of job opportunities, and a high job-migration rate; and we decided that we must concentrate in one area: the city.

But I raised my voice to say "No," because the people who make up the city come from the small and outlying areas. They come from the Deep South, and we can even go back and trace migratory patterns from Williamsburg, South Carolina over a period of years, and show you that these migrants make up part of the population in Rochester. If we want we can take the statistical data and find that anyone in New York City who migrates from North Carolina goes primarily to one area of Brooklyn or north of 135th Street in Manhattan, where the sons and daughters of North Carolina have an organization that functions regularly. We can also trace the migratory pattern from Virginia to various towns. These studies now bear out what I have been saying all along. In order to really deal with American society—and I believe that we are all Americans; I am not one of those who believes we should go back to Africa; my fate is right here—we must look at rural economic development as a means of dealing with the problem of housing. The development of Soul City comes out of these basic beliefs.

So when you ask the question, "Are New Towns for Lower Income Americans Too?" I say, that depends upon the new town and it depends upon its objectives. I think a man could build a new town without being concerned about integrated housing. I think many new communities, as that term is broadly interpreted, can just include subdevelopments, which allow people to escape their responsibilities in the cities and create more problems by moving out into the suburbs, permitting the city to become a city with no economic base, which then requires large expenditures. The tax base has been eroded, a continual migratory pattern comes in to play, and you have urban unrest and you have drugs.

I think that we really have to deal with the totality of American problems, and I see the new communities legislation of 1968 as a vehicle for really solving these problems. For that reason I concentrated my efforts, went back to my home base in North Carolina, and started working on this particular project—to really develop a concept by which we could solve American problems. Economic development is the main barrier that must be penetrated, and the new town itself affords an opportunity for this penetration.

But first let me give you a little background on Soul City. Soul City is located in the county of Warren, about 17 miles south of the North Carolina-Virginia line. You can drive from Washington in three hours because we're located between two interstate highways, 95 and

85. The Seaboard Railroad comes through our property; and so does U.S. Highway 1, the old road created at the time of the 13 original colonies, which was once called the Boston Post Road.

We are in the Black Belt. We didn't make it the Black Belt; it was already there. We didn't bring the people there, and we didn't create slavery, but we know that this area has an extraordinarily high out-migration. You can go back and look at the transportation records and you will find that the day after high school graduation, 75 percent of the kids get on a Greyhound bus, a Trailway bus—or they get on the train and they move north. They move northward having finished an inferior high school education, to seek employment in the land of opportunity; they move to the great metropolitan area, which says "Here is where we want you and you've got the opportunity to move forward." Once they get there they become disillusioned. So this is the place where Soul City is located.

The average income? You can get the community profile, and you will find that in 1970 the average income per family was less than $3,000 per year. Here is the source of our problem, our reason for migration. There are lots of economic opportunities in the North, and there are thousands of dead cities in the South: when we say thousands of dead cities, just look at your map. Also, look at the decline in agriculture because of the cost of farm labor and the cost of machinery and equipment, which have been rapidly rising. Many of these towns existed because they were based on an agricultural economy. Throughout North Carolina, South Carolina, Georgia, and all the other southern states we find dying towns, towns that are mere names on a road map, exhibiting little or no activity.

It was our idea to go right back into this area because it is a beautiful area—beautiful, sloping, rolling hills. It is not isolated: there are 32 schools and colleges within a radius of 100 miles from Soul City. Soul City is easily accessible, and we cooperate with the University of North Carolina, Raleigh and Chapel Hill particularly (it is a state institution), and North Carolina College, at Durham.

We went into this area, and after we acquired the land we found the governor responsive. At that time the governor designated Regional Planning Areas of the state, and we became Region K. We started to develop Soul City in 1969, not only to build Soul City itself, but to coordinate its development with the development of the entire region, which had a water shortage, great economic problems, and a population that was a combination of Indians, poor whites, and blacks. You can believe me, anytime in the South that you have a high outward migratory rate for blacks, you likewise have a high migratory rate for whites and for Indians. It is for this reason that Soul City was conceived. We decided that here was the area where a free-standing new community should be built.

We believed further that in order to stop the migration north we would have to create job opportunities. To do this we would have to do comprehensive planning. We planned and studied every conceivable problem. We studied growth patterns: how many babies the people are going to have, and how to raise the income of the people so they can buy what they need. We have developed a great big book of assumptions, and one of our assumptions is that these people cannot buy homes with the incomes that they now have. Our effort will have to focus on raising the income of these people in order for them to have adequate housing.

Another of our assumptions has been this: At the same time we create opportunities for these people, we can create a kind of economic model that will interest outside investors and industrialists, but will not conflict with our determination to bring about a mix so that we can develop a community allowing for people to develop to their utmost. We created a planning base involving the citizens of the region, and blacks, whites, and Indians have been included in our planning process from the outset.

Just recently we won a bond issue election for a regional water system. We brought together three counties: Vance County, where Henderson, North Carolina is located; Granville County, where Oxford is located; and Warren County, where Soul City is located. If you were driving up the Interstate from Raleigh-Durham, when you got to the Granville county line you would see a great big sign up there: "The Ku Klux Klan of Granville County Welcomes You." We went down there three years ago and we found that you have to appeal to people's self-interest. We decided that we could fight every battle that came forth, but that we would have to narrow our focus if we were going to whip the people together in this region. There were people there who really wanted to work, so we got together and developed a regional water system. We finally got them all together last year, when the three counties and the three municipalities (and you can imagine how many meetings we had over a period of three years) entered into a signed agreement.

Next we had to get funding for the water system, and we went to each of the councils and county commissioners and finally put it together. The financing of this system required a bond issue in two towns: Henderson and Oxford. Oxford had to get the citizens to approve a bond issue of about $800,000, close to $1 million now. And the town of Henderson had to have a bond issue of better than $2 million.

Just before the election I spoke at the First Baptist Church in Oxford, and my subject was the Psychology of the Mule. I started from Isaiah, which says, "A whip for the horse, a girdle and a bit for the mule, and a rod for the fool," and that was my text to encourage people to get out and vote in favor of a water issue to save that area. And they did. Of course, I really do preach every now and then; I just spoke the other day and I got one of those weird texts from Ecclesiastes; it says, "Wine is for the feast, laughter maketh merry, but money solveth all things." That becomes one of my speeches also.

So Soul City is a regional concept. We use Soul City to do what we've always thought we could do: bring blacks and whites and Indians together in this community and really build a kind of society that can say to America: "Look, we may be predominantly black, but we bet you that we can treat you better than you have treated us. We bet you that we can bring people together to work constructively if we use one motivating force, that of self-interest. We bet you that we can plan together, and we bet you that we can build the kind of society that can actually help the city solve its problems by involving people in the planning process."

Now, we could talk all day about Soul City, but I don't want to talk all day about Soul City, I want to offer you the opportunity to ask me about Soul City. Before that, however, I would like to conclude by getting back to economic development. Our first interest is to create the employment base for Soul City. I think right now if you went to Fortune's 1,000 businesses in the United States, you would not find a single black business listed, and that means American society has a long way to go. In creating an industrial base for Soul City, partnerships can be established with businesses. In our first three-year plan we have already attracted three industries. The first will bring in 350 jobs. This commitment helped stimulate a second company to commit itself, a company that supplies wood chips to other industries. This gives us 400 jobs within our first two years. This has a multiplying effect: according to our economists these 400 basic jobs will create at least 800 support jobs, bringing us up to 1,200 jobs within this short period of time.

Being in an agricultural community, we are encouraging blacks and whites to join together to engage in other ventures in the development of Soul City. Our first building process is homes. We are in a poor community to start with, you see. We don't have the same concerns you would have at any of the other new towns that are being considered here. We have a real problem of restructuring attitudes. We have a problem of economic and industrial development.

We hope to sell our new town bonds sometime after the close of the fiscal year. At the time that we sell our bonds, we will have resolved the question for the free-standing community of which comes first, the chicken or the egg. The residents around Soul City told us when we had a community meeting at the outset that the first thing they wanted was health services. We do not have nearly enough doctors in this area. So we immediately got a grant to do our planning in the area of health. We packaged a deal and we got $1.1 million from the Office of Economic Opportunity for health services. We recruited half of the staff of Harlem Hospital, headed by Dr. Stanford Roman; they will be on site in Soul City, and building plans have already begun.

Two industrial plants will be started, and we have just received funds for our first industrial incubator plant; this is called "Soultech I" and will house our first industry. An industrial incubator plant is a plant that any factory can move into immediately and start production, during which time training processes can go on. We have fortunately been able to persuade many of the federal agencies to commit themselves to coordinated training.

The State of North Carolina, through the State Planning Office, is intimately involved in our project. We now do most of the planning for the region—it wasn't intended that way but it ends up being that way—we have an office and a staff, and we can plan for the region based upon the original work that we did during our first year.

Soul City is moving along. After the sale of the bonds, housing construction will immediately commence: single-family housing, garden apartments, housing on the lake, schools, a shopping center, and an office building, all conceived within our first-year plan. Just providing housing is not the answer; we believe that providing the incomes to occupy the housing comes first.

Discussion

HASS: I came from the Appalachian Mountains coal mining areas and I want to ask what safeguards can be built into Soul City as well as other new towns to keep them from becoming company towns. This was the scourge of a generation ago throughout the mountains.

McKISSICK: I think there are a number of safeguards. I believe the major safeguards lie in an educated population, and I think that America has progressed in this regard. From the example of the 1960s uprisings, we have a far more educated population. The people criticize; they have the ability to criticize. Reading ability has also increased. Expanded public education is really the answer. I also think federal laws now add many protections.

Also, I think that in new towns you've got the developer himself. New community leaders, in spite of the fact that each builds in a different locality, have a sense of morality that I'm impressed with; I've found that true in all the new town developers I have worked with; they no longer have the attitudes of the 1920s.

I think that racism is on the wane in this country. I don't mean that it's gone, but I do think that there have been some positive changes, and I think if we really can rid ourselves of negative attitudes and concentrate on the positive, pull people together on positive attitudes, and keep an educated public moving forward, the chance of any community being dominated by one company is remote, today.

HASS: Well, I'm not sure this is enough. Columbia, Maryland, despite the fine dreams of Mr. Rouse, is slowly pulling back from its original commitment because of the big industries that have moved in.

McKISSICK: Well, I don't know all the details of Columbia but I do know that my key staff spent about a month up there in training. To believe that new communities are not going to have some of the problems that other communities have is fallacious reasoning. I think that we will have them. For example, in our community right now we don't have the problem of drugs. But we're doing planning for drug abuse, because we don't ever want to have that problem. The advantage that we have—there is no guarantee—but the advantage that we have in a new community is that we can recognize problems and start planning for them now. I think a free-standing new community has an advantage over Columbia in the first place. I think we're building attitudes in the new community; we're building people; we're doing something that I don't think could be done in a new-town-in-town.

I have faith in the changing attitudes of the region. A great change has already come about, just in the support for Soul City. When we first arrived there was a completely negative attitude toward Soul City, and now five counties are working with us even though one still has the sign that reads: "The Ku Klux Klan Welcomes You." The other night at a regional meeting we had 50 percent black and 50 percent white sitting down talking rationally about how to solve some of their problems.

I just don't want to give up; I believe in sound economics, and I don't believe conservatism is racism. I believe that people are now changing; I think we are living in a new day. And as for one-company control of a town, I just don't believe it would ever be possible at Soul City because we are trying very hard to get people to question everything that comes about, even us. We find that we grow in that process.

SUSSMAN: I want to pursue Reverend Hass's point. I don't see Columbia as a company town so much in terms of the industries that have located there, but more in terms of the research and development company that is the developer of Columbia. It owns almost all of the commercial real estate, a lot of the industrial real estate, and some of the enterprises themselves within the city. That's the characteristic of a company town; that is, the economic health of the town is controlled by a single company. I was wondering how it would be different in Soul City.

McKISSICK: McKissick Enterprises is the developer of Soul City, but McKissick Enterprises continues to throw off its responsibilities to other companies and entities. For example, we started when my wife permitted me to mortgage our property to get our first $50,000. And then, because we were firm believers in social planning, our first act was to create the Soul City Foundation, a 501-C3 corporation. That corporation now has total responsibility for the social planning at Soul City. Sometimes McKissick Enterprises argues with the Soul City Foundation; that's natural and to be expected in growth.

We then created the Warren Regional Planning Corporation, another corporation, to assume the responsibility for the technical development and research plan. That is where the planning is done for the total community under the auspices of 701 planning funds through HUD and the State of North Carolina planning funds. In cooperation with their office we do the physical planning; the architects and engineers are in that corporation and that kind of responsibility is thrown off.

Thirdly, we moved to create a Soul City Investment Company at the same time the Soul City Foundation was created, so that citizens can own a piece of the action in Soul City. The employees of the company and people in the five-county area invest in this company; had they not invested we'd have serious problems. We went into an area where there was no electricity or any other kind of utility; there were only five long-distance lines out of the county. With the help of their investment utilities are now being established.

I think under the New Communities Act and legislation, the developer of a new community, in signing an agreement with HUD, agrees to follow a development plan; but I think a reading of the development plan will show that there is a gradual turning of controls over to other instrumentalities. For example, we now have created the Soul City Sanitary District, which is responsible for sewers and waste and what not. It is working on an innovative process of spray sewers to make it possible for the land to be used in cooperation with a farming corporation called the Foundation for Community Development, ANDAMULE. They now farm our land.

By various other contracts we're doing more innovative things. I don't fear people and I don't think they have to be controlled by one big corporation that stands over them; I think it's a process of educating, and that people will respond accordingly when they see it's for their own good. And I also think that when we throw out these kinds of questions, we're thinking about what used to be out there.

I'm saying that free-standing communities destroy 50 percent of those old concepts. Have you ever seen this ad on TV and radio? "All aspirin is alike. . ." Well, we're overthrowing some of the old basic concepts in a free community. We throw the ball to many organizations in regard to land use and planning. They've given us a mandate to do some of these things for them and they want us to control it to do it for them.

Our situation is entirely different from that of Columbia's research and development corporation. We didn't acquire our land in the same way; neither did we have the money the Rouse Company has. In fact, we had to borrow the shoestring. I think that we are living in a new day; free-standing new communities overcome 50 percent of those problems.

HAGER: I'd like to follow through on the economic development you were speaking of earlier. I assume that these new industries that are coming in are from relatively larger corporations from the outside. Are you doing anything to develop indigenous smaller industry, minority industry, and in that process are you making any cooperatives?

McKISSICK: The answer is yes. However, the word, "cooperative" has been giving me a problem since I got through looking at one charging people about 15 percent interest, when we could set up a corporation and charge 6 percent; the value of that magic word "cooperative" as what it used to be years ago has faded from my mind. The question is: how does it actually function, and what do people pay for money? If a cooperative is going to lend money at twice the rate that you can get money from a local development company, or something else, then I don't run to that name just because it's "cooperative." I look at the roles people play and then make a decision.

As for other problems, bringing our offices to Soul City created some headaches, but flexibility helped us resolve them. We had a little problem with HUD in getting black appraisers to appraise our land. We finally got Jones and Darby of New York, who were finally admitted to the American Appraisers Association, and HUD approved this; but Jones and Darby were not there to start off with. We had a second problem telling the phone company, "Look, if we're going to have all these phones out here and we're going to be laying down all these lines, you have to get some blacks on the crew." They said, "We can't." We said, "You can." And we won out. We've had all kinds of such problems, but we've solved them.

We now have two construction companies. Two—we don't believe one construction company could build Soul City. Our medical center will be built by a minority company. On the other hand, when skills are needed, we're not just hiring people because they grow their hair long or holler Black Power. We're going to hire the man that knows how to put this thing together. We're going to ask him to take a young black or a young Indian along with him and give him training and skill. This is part of our program.

We have an affirmative action program. Our population ratio is about 65 percent black, 5 percent Indian, and the remainder white. At a board meeting our members agreed we should have a white affirmative action officer rather than a black one in our project. I've been knocking folks over the head for years now to follow the Civil Rights Act, and it's no more than right that they insist that I follow it too. These are the kinds of decisions that we are able to make because we have people of a quality that will make them the real new builders of American Society.

We have developed three minority businesses in Soul City. We do not have the name of "co-op" on anything as yet, but we do emphasize that everybody should buy a piece of the land, not rent it; we are trying to emphasize buying.

When we deal with industrialists we sit down and we negotiate with each industrialist. We have learned that it's easy to make a general rule, but that the general rule never seems to apply because there are more exceptions to the rule than actual applications of it. So we go and sit down with an industry and we say, "Look, we want you in here," and most industries, we have found, say, "We are sold on the industrial studies of Soul City; what we're worried about is your educational system, what we're worried about is how blacks and whites get along together." Those are the key questions that industrialists have asked us. We sit down and we cut a deal with them. We say, "You're going to bring 50 people down here on some date and we want to have this training program set up by that date." We involve the technical institutes of the State of North Carolina to coordinate a program. This has been our method. We say we're going to have a health center and we want everybody that's going to be employed there enrolled in that health center. This is a major problem. We sit down and negotiate and ask what kind of profit-sharing plan they have for their employees. I think American society has come a longer way than many of us want to acknowledge. I also think we concentrate too much on our pessimists.

GREENDALE: Do you see whites coming into Soul City? What's your projection on that?

McKISSICK: Yes, we see white people coming into Soul City. In fact, I would say that the town is going to end up being about 50-50, and that will be in the next four to five years. That's our projection.

Incidentally, someone was asking me last night, "If your town is open to all people, why name it Soul City?" I said that maybe I was under a false impression, but I thought white people had souls too. Soul is a religious concept; you look at Los Angeles, its real name is "The City of Angels." Right now on our staff team, for example, we have more white applicants for jobs in the skilled categories. That's an indication of what has been happening in that part of society.

I think Soul City is going to become a very important research town. We've had a number of people who've come down in the field of transportation. At least 17 colleges and universities work with us on various phases of the program.

Soul City affords an opportunity for people who are really concerned. We have a number of integrated married couples, many of them returning from the war, who want to come in. I really think Soul City is going to set a pattern that will transcend the racism existing in other places. Whites will be totally involved. We know a number of couples from the University of North Carolina area who would like to move in now and just live in mobile homes, as our staff is living. The Soul City Investment Corporation keeps adding to its mobile units. Our affirmative action officer is always saying, "Let's bring them in," and we always add, "Yes, bring them on in." And this is what happens.

DEUTSCHMAN: I thank you for bringing us to the point where I feel that we might be getting close to a substantive issue this morning. When you begin to deal with the economics in Columbia, it's a lot of fun to blame HUD, or Jim Rouse, or outside industry, or what have you. But somehow it seems to me that we're getting close to dealing with the profit motive and capitalism, which are in this whole bag. It seems to me that we're getting close to dealing with the will of the American people to do something about housing for the poor people with a more than token approach. In Columbia we have low income subsidized housing. However, if the residents in this housing improve their financial situation a bit, there's no place for them to move to in Columbia. I can't blame Rouse. There is no money available for further subsidized programs for in-between stages. Capitalism has forced the market up to where a townhouse in my unit that was built three-and-a-half years ago and sold then for $16,000, sold last week for $32,000. I guess I feel—and I'd like your response to this—that unless we get to the point where we have a federal land use policy, and a federal massive approach to low income housing, we're not going to get anywhere, and that's true for HUD new communities as well as private new communities.

McKISSICK: I think you are absolutely correct. I believe that the New Communities Act needs a tremendous amount more; but I think it is a start. The New Communities Act needs tremendous resources and more power, and it must develop a national land use act. I think the concept of regionalism is a start; when we talk of federalism we sometimes separate the government from its power to deal with various political subdivisions. You are saying something we just got through talking about two weeks ago, that the New Communities program has to move forward toward a national land use program. For example, I can even see how under such a program you could work cooperatively with the Department of Agriculture if you have, say, a crisis in soy beans or floods in Mississippi. There are thousands of acres that could be cultivated in substitution for the flooded lands in Mississippi, and this could change the economics of the country. I think we've also got to move in that direction with people and housing and the good old concept of moving America forward.

CHAPTER 4

LEGISLATIVE FRONTIERS: LOWER INCOME AMERICANS AND NEW TOWNS
Hugh Mields, Jr.

In the American lexicon "frontiers" are always identified with challenge. So, when we talk about a legislative frontier, we are really talking about a legislative challenge—and this may be the year that the forces of good, and I say that in the most generous way that I can, are going to face challenges beyond belief. The 235 and 236 interest-subsidy programs are in a state of suspension by the Administration on the grounds that they don't really work for the people for whom they were intended. A whole series of categorical aid programs, such as water and sewer, neighborhood facilities, and renewal, which were largely designed to provide supportive facilities for housing and for good neighborhoods, have been terminated by the Administration on the grounds that you can't solve problems by throwing money at them. This is sort of an unholy comment, isn't it, since we have been told by Mr. McKissick that the Bible says, "Money solveth all things."

The public housing program is on the brink of financial disaster because tenant incomes are too low, as are welfare allowances, to pay rents sufficient to cover the interest and principal costs, much less maintenance and periodic rehabilitation. The unhappy state of this 35-year-old program is further exacerbated by growing numbers of vacancies; this is the direct result of bad management, bad maintenance, and bad behavior. The growing level of social disorganization within public housing projects is largely attributable to the inordinate concentration of welfare families. Congress is waiting anxiously for the Administration housing proposals, which are not due until the fall; and I'll be surprised if the Administration makes its own time limit. In the meantime housing starts are down, housing prices are up; and the lower income Americans are left, as is usually the case, holding the short end of the stick.

Now, how does this relate to new towns? Let me say that I think new towns, especially Title VII new towns, are for lower-income

Americans too. In passing on the Urban Growth and New Communities Development Act of 1970, Congress made a series of findings, from which I have excerpted the following, which are related to housing issues:

> Continuation of established patterns of urban development, together with anticipated increases in population, will unduly limit the options for many of our people about where they may live and the types of housing and environments in which they may live. There will also be less opportunity for the private homebuilding industry to operate at its highest potential capacity and provide the good housing needed to serve an expanded population and to replace substandard housing. There will be further lessening of employment and business opportunities for the residents of central cities, and the ability of such cities to retain a tax base adequate to support vital services for all their citizens, particularly the poor and disadvantaged, will be further impaired.
>
> Better patterns of urban development and revitalization are essential to accommodate further population growth, to prevent further deterioration of the nation's physical and social environment, and to make a positive contribution to improving the overall quality of life in the nation. The national welfare requires the encouragement of well-planned, diversified, and economically sound new communities and major additions to existing communities as one of the several essential elements of a consistent national program for bettering patterns of development and renewal.
>
> It is the purpose of Title VII to provide private developers and state and local public bodies and agencies with the financial and other assistance necessary to encourage the orderly development of well-planned, diversified, economically sound new communities, which would, among other things, increase for all persons, particularly members of minority groups, the available choices of locations for living and working, thereby providing for a more just, economic, and social environment. Other purposes of the act are to assist in the efficient production of a steady supply of residential, commercial, and industrial sites at a reasonable cost; to increase the ability of the home-building industry to utilize new technology; and to produce the large volumes of well-designed, inexpensive housing needed to accommodate future growth.

Only those new community development programs that make a substantial provision for housing within the means of persons of low and moderate income, and such housing will constitute an appropriate portion of a community's housing supply, will be considered as eligible for assistance under the provisions of federal law.

My experience has been that a large number of people who talk knowledgeably about Title VII have never actually read the bill and have only a slight comprehension of what's contained in it and what the intention of Congress was. I sometimes think, in all deference to Edward Lamont, that we don't have enough guys in the federal government who read what the intentions of Congress are. To date, this Administration doesn't worry too much about what Congress thinks.

What has been the response to this particular mandate? Ted Lamont has given you the numbers; mine are a little different, and I think my numbers may be a little outdated, since I picked them up from the fact sheets when they were released as the 15 new communities were approved by HUD for guarantees. But let me tell you mine; they're not that different: to some extent they're a little more conservative and to some extent they're a little more optimistic.

The fifteen new communities that have been approved are in nine states. When they are completed they will house well over .5 million people in about 270,000 dwelling units. Approximately 108,000 of the new dwelling units are expected to be available for low and moderate income families. Now, by my numbers this constitutes about 40 percent of the new housing units that will be constructed in the new communities over the next 18 to about 25 years (these various new towns have different development periods).

Despite my introduction I think the future of this program looks reasonably good. The Administration actually and honestly has indicated that the program should continue—it's one of those programs that survived. The budget for 1974, as Ted has indicated, looks to an approval of 14 to 16 new communities by the start of 1975. They talk about 20 new communities, and a few of them have been approved already. Also, the Administration has indicated that Title VII-approved new communities will not be subject to the current housing moratorium. Now, it's not clear, and maybe Ted will want to comment, how HUD intends to provide the waivers. But if it means that HUD fully intends to meet its contractual obligations under existing project agreements with these 15 new towns, then all of the new towns underway that have projected construction of federally assisted 235 or 236 units during the next year and a half should receive the necessary moratorium waivers for the housing units they require and get the units when they require them. Now, as I say, although we think that the moratorium will be waived for them, we still have to see more concrete evidence of that fact.

In terms of the projections that are being made by the developers, at this point I don't know of any community developer that proposes to use the public housing program to help meet his housing commitment. I think probably if the public housing program survives, and I'm not sure that it will, some of the new town developers may use it to provide housing for the aged. And I would also guess that some of them will try to use some of the Section 23 leased housing available through the public housing program. And as a matter of fact, after having said it, I do believe that Cedar-Riverside is using leased housing now through the public housing authority. But in any event, I see no prospect for the construction of traditional public housing projects in Title VII new communities, and I think the reasons are obvious.

In terms of the new town developers' intention to meet reasonable low and moderate income housing goals, the record of the Title VII—and I'm talking about intentions—looks good. In fact, I think those numbers are unique and outstanding. There isn't any other kind of development of any scale going on in the United States today that comes anywhere near matching them in terms of the proportion and the supporting facilities the new town developers propose to provide. And I think the intentions are good, because new town developers face some really tough problems in aggregating the resources necessary to make this kind of housing in their new communities feasible. For example, at this juncture we have no real idea what sort of assisted housing program the Administration will support. HUD's program recommendations will not be made available, as we've indicated, to the public or the Congress until this fall. Whatever the Administration decides and whatever Congress agrees to, however, I think we can be relatively sure that funds for housing for lower income Americans will continue to fall considerably short of meeting the actual need, because the level of subsidies that will probably be made available simply will not be adequate.

I think this means that supporters of the New Towns program will seek some preferential treatment from Congress in terms of an allocation or of an assurance of an annual allocation of federal housing resources, probably as well as grants for supporting public facilities. And we hope, and here I associate myself with the supporters of the program, that Congress will agree to an annual allocation sufficient to meet the target set in the law itself.

Project agreements are contracts between the developer and HUD in which the developer promises to deliver the number of units set forth. In return HUD sometimes obligates itself to provide the actual subsidies for the housing, but this reciprocity is dubious at this point. We hope that as the program progresses the certainty about the obligations of the developer will be reflected by an equal amount of certainty about the actions of HUD.

If the Congress does agree to such an allocation, and if the Administration decides to abide by the intent of Congress and actually set aside part of the total allocation of federal housing assistance to new communities, the potential of this program for delivering housing to modest income Americans will, in my view, be substantially augmented. I see it as a tremendous opportunity.

However, it is possible, for a variety of reasons, that some opposition in the Congress to such a set-aside might develop. For example, if housing subsidy funds will be in relatively short supply, and they probably will be, then it's reasonable to assume that there will be opposition to a new town set-aside. Again, the developers and builders would undoubtedly prefer freedom to use the program wherever cheap land is available, which most likely means peripheral tract development; public agencies, on the other hand, will be seeking all the subsidized units they can get and will probably want them for relatively small inner city projects. The way the concept fares in the Congress will depend largely on how effectively the new town developers use the housing subsidies allocations they already have. I think that in the next few years the kind of track record they develop will have a tremendous impact on how Congress and the Administration will respond with additional assistance.

Ted (Lamont), I hope next year at this time, when somebody asks you about what's happening in new towns, you can come up with a lot more numbers in terms of units built and a good solid proportion of low and moderate and minority group housing. And I believe those numbers will be available. I think the program is moving.

In this regard, though, it should be pointed out that a new town developer takes on some very difficult problems when assuming a contractual obligation to provide housing for the proportion of lower-income families existing in the metropolitan area in which the new town is being built. In almost every case that I know of, the new community developer has found it necessary to subsidize the cost of land in order to make the units economically feasible. The developer is also obligated under the law to make certain that all the families in the new community receive or have full access to a relatively full complement of social services and facilities. When evaluating the potential ability of any developer to deliver this kind of housing in new communities, it is important to remember that the initial cost of providing housing is only one aspect of the problem. The low and moderate income housing unit, as well as all the other dwellings in the new community, has to have an adequate level of public services and facilities, plus whatever extra amenity package may have to be developed to make the community marketable to the families he's trying to attract into the community itself. Since existing local governments are seldom—that's the wrong word, they're never—ready to make such investments in infrastructure, this generally means that the developer must assume the burden of financing public facilities entirely on his own and early on. Special assessments usually have to be levied on a communitywide basis to pay for the extra facilities and services needed to make the new town competitive. The assessments are usually handled by a community association or a homeowners' association, or whatever other institutional device is created by the developer and HUD to operate, control, and insure the delivery of amenities and services that are a necessary part of the new community and a part of the project agreement that the developer has with HUD. This may very well pose a problem in the future in persuading the middle- and upper-middle and upper-income families, as well as commerce and industry, that are to be a part of the new community, to assume the extra monetary burdens required to carry the lower-income groups that will be living there.

New communities are designed to be self-sufficient. They get very little help from the outside, at this point, from the state and local governments within which they are being built. The obligation of the federal government is the critical issue. I'm sure you all know, and it's already been alluded to at this consultation, that economic integration is absolutely the most difficult kind of thing to accomplish in a competitive setting. New towns will be pioneering in this kind of integration, and nobody anticipates it to be an easy process. New town developers assume a special burden in this respect: they're obligated under the law to assure the provisions of these services and facilities. I'm sorry to keep repeating this, but I think it is terribly important. HUD and the federal government, as well as state and local governments, have made no special effort up to this point to supply supporting services or otherwise assist the developers to achieve this important objective. I think probably Soul City has done better than most in terms of getting special assistance, and I'm very much Mr. McKissick's admirer for it; I think it was a monumental job. Also, new towns developers themselves are not getting any special assistance, although I believe they should, in planning innovative programs and exploring the potential sources of financing for these programs.

Title VII authorized a whole series of grants, including public service grants to help provide the necessary public services and facilities early on in a project when there are too few residents to support them adequately. This Administration has never requested one nickel from Congress to carry out that particular objective of the act.

Title VII also authorized special planning grants to private as well as public developers, to enable them to study the uses of new technology and learn how to apply new and improved social service delivery systems to new towns. Supporters of this program managed to get Congress to appropriate $5 million for that purpose, but HUD refused to make the money available.

In order to encourage more public involvement in the program, Title VII authorized interest differential grants, by which public bodies could use the HUD guarantee to float bonds that would not be tax-exempt; in order to make the interest attractive they could subsidize the difference between what it would have cost them if they had gone tax-exempt and what it did cost them to go with a non-tax-exempt bond. That program has never been implemented.

HUD has authority to undertake technical assistance to state and local governments and to private developers, as well as to non-profit organizations or cooperatives if they're interested in pursuing the objectives of this program. The Administration has not made any effort to request funds from the Congress to carry out this particular function; the law and Congress intended that they do it, but they haven't. The Office of New Community Development (ONCD) has operated on a shoestring, and it's a constant source of amazement to me that we actually have a program and that 15 new communities have been approved. On the basis of the numbers we have had to deal with in supporting this program since its inception, it's really a fantastic achievement.

Also, there is a false impression—and some evidence of it has emerged in this meeting, and this is a very broad kind of impression that many people have—that developers are sharp traders, that when developers speak of the need for grants they are really just looking for handouts, and that all the developers want is to augment what will obviously be a fantastically profitable enterprise. That impression is totally undeserved, or I should say, largely undeserved, in the case of new town developers. I have no experience with other developers so I won't stand in defense of their motivations or intentions, but in my opinion the developers who have assumed obligations to build new communities under Title VII are dedicated people who are really interested in building new cities and meeting the social objectives of the Title VII programs in the process. But this bias, which touches the federal administration and others who are observers of the program, has made it pretty tough for good developers to persuade the Administration that this extra level of assistance is necessary to assure the provision of social services to meet the health and educational needs of the lower income families who are going to be living in Title VII new towns.

Finally, there is another problem, and I think most of you are aware of it. In our urban areas there is an increasing sentiment against growth. Efforts are made to slow or stop growth, and many of these efforts are made by people who are sincerely motivated by a desire to protect the environment. But then there are also some who, since they just got located on a three-acre lot and like it the way it is, would prefer that nothing else happen. I'm not going to comment any more on that than to say that in many of our more rapidly growing metropolitan areas this no-growth and slow-growth sentiment has severely hampered the whole business of providing housing for lower income people to a point where people with incomes of less than $15,000 don't even think about buying a house, it's out of the question. In the Washington area, the average value of housing in Montgomery and Fairfax counties is well over $40,000 and going up.

Since I tried to play a bit of an advocate role here in terms of the new communities program, I'd like to thank Dave Blue, who was invited and who was formerly with ONCD and who is now a private consultant, for some of these ideas. He set forth some reasons why people who are interested in augmenting the supply of low income housing should support new communities. I think I want to make this caveat first, that I don't know of anybody who does expect new towns to provide a panacea for the really highly complex problem of dealing with the total needs of our low and moderate income families. But new towns do, I think, provide a set of conditions that potentially can obviate many of the difficulties that we face in trying to provide suitable low cost housing for poor and moderate income families. In any event these are some of the reasons why I think that the program deserves your support:

1. New communities stress total community planning and large tracts, with a balance of different kinds of housing that can be physically and socially integrated into a total community.

2. New communities provide a basis for establishing and maintaining high design and quality standards for all types of housing and for reducing the labeling of low and moderate income housing as such.

3. New communities are concerned with the adequacy of the employment base as well as with housing. They provide a means for relating employment needs and potential to housing needs and integrating manpower-training programs with such needs on a long-term basis.

4. New communities seek to make adequate provision for comprehensively planned health, day-care, educational, cultural, and recreational programs to meet the needs of the various groups in the community at a cost level suitable to those groups and in a manner consistent with overall community objectives.

5. To the extent that the developers are required to commit themselves to proportions of low and moderate income housing in a community, there is redistribution of capital that in effect takes place in the initial steps of community planning.

The developer must direct his efforts toward providing such housing at an acceptable cost level for the people who will be using it; he will in effect be subsidizing this housing through a variety of means, hidden and overt, including government housing subsidies (we hope), and also including his own land write-downs, economy of scale, and other favorable features of the new communities financing and planning process. The potential for reducing housing costs is also present in new community settings because of the high-volume, long-term nature of this kind of housing production. This creates special possibilities not only for significant economies of scale but for a variety of industrialized housing techniques and for generally economical planning. Presumably the problems of zoning and restrictive land use, and of squabbling among different levels of government, are also precluded once the new community approval is given, but not always.

The new community is one of the few alternatives to the fragmented, discordant approaches that have characterized efforts to meet the need for housing of moderate and low income Americans in the past.

Now, having said all that, let me speak just a minute about land use legislation. There are currently two bills pending before the Congress. One is before Senator Jackson's committee, the Interior Committee of the Senate. It is a mélange of ideas that relate to the problem of developing state-wide land use programs; in my view it is not a particularly well-organized piece of legislation, and it is not one that relates to the problem we are discussing here today. As a matter of fact it is essentially an environmental protection bill, with strong antidevelopment implications. It simply provides a series of grants to states over a five-year period to enable them to undertake the development of comprehensive land use control programs. The legislation sets certain kinds of objectives for such programs, but no substantive set of standards is established. In its organization and in fixing the responsibilities the states must assume in order to qualify for this assistance, the Department of Interior is involved, HUD is involved, the Council of Environmental Quality is involved; when you get through reading it you're not quite sure who is going to have responsibility for what, when, and under what circumstances. It is, in my view, bad legislation. If I were voting on the floor I'd vote against it.

On the House side, I don't know what Congressman Udall is proposing in the Interior Committee. He has promised he will get a bill out, and I suspect that it will be a better organized one, since I don't think he's susceptible to some of the pressures the Senate committee has had to deal with.

The bill as originally introduced by the Administration, and in this instance I have to agree with the Administration's view, included sanctions that said if a state did not develop a suitable land use program after three years of assistance there would be applied, on a cumulative basis, 7 percent reduction on airport money, 7 percent reduction on highway money, and 7 percent reduction on land and water conservation grant funds. This would add up to a total of 21 percent, which would hold as long as the state refused or was incapable of developing an adequate and acceptable land use program. This was not, as I understand it, in the bill that was reported to the Senate, although Senator Jackson said he would introduce an amendment on the floor, although that same provision was defeated on the floor of the Senate last year. But I do think that these sanctions and the inclusion of substantive standards for land use programs are pretty essential. I also think basic responsibility for administering the program has got to be fixed on one place and that whoever gets it, be it Interior or HUD or the Domestic Council, has got to have some sticks as well as some carrots to get the states to make some sense with the way we're consuming land in this country. I don't want you to think that I think the thing has been a totally useless exercise; it hasn't. But I am mostly disappointed and opposed to it, since once this legislation has passed the Congress everyone will assume that what is necessary to be done has been done. Years will pass, until at the end of the fourth or beginning of the fifth year we will discover that it hasn't worked, that nobody has been mandated to do anything, and that nobody has really followed through.

Discussion

HANSEN: I work for a regional planning body called the Tri-State Regional Planning Commission. We have studied possible new communities in the urbanized portions of Connecticut, New York, and New Jersey. Except for some very large tracts of land, such as the Stewart Air Force Base, which isn't available anymore, and Floyd Bennett Air Field, which is now part of Gateway National Park, new communities don't really seem to be useful in getting low income people integrated into this society. The Planned Urban Development (PUD) concept is probably the most viable kind of development in our region in terms of integrating blacks and whites.

As a matter of fact, George Sternlieb at the Rutgers Center found that PUDs were able to get a much higher proportion of blacks into new developments than there is in standard subdivisions. I'd like to follow this observation with another one; namely that the federal government should set aside money for planned urban developments.

One of the problems we face in Section 235 funding, for instance, is that this program has received only 1 percent of the nation's funding, although the group it represents comes close to 10 percent of the country's population. Further, the section 235 houses that have been built have been rehabilitations for the most part, with many of them located in far-out settings such as Suffolk County and parts of New Jersey. We have a problem, therefore, of not really being able to direct subsidies for low income people in the suburbs, plus the fact that there are so many barriers to this program. What I would like to know is whether or not PUDs, or some form of PUDs that are really mini-new-communities, could be developed as a federal goal.

MIELDS: They could and probably will during this year's legislation. The Homebuilders are in favor of what they call Planned Neighborhood Developments, and I know there's some sympathy for this approach in the Banking Committee on the House side. I think there's no question about the desirability of that kind of planned development for in-filling, and for smaller developments that really complement the area in which they are located. Basically, they achieve the objectives of Title VII.

I think the question is, to what extent can Title VII, as it's presently organized and constituted, actually accommodate the kinds of market it would develop? There is a lot of interest in the kind of scale you're talking about, and it also applies to slow-growing metropolitan areas where absorption rates are maybe 200, 300, or 400 acres a year, which you may wish to extend to maybe 300, 500, or 800 acres of development in order to complement the adjacent area. There is interest in this kind of a program. I think it's a good idea and I hope we can do something with it, and I hope we can get the Administration to agree to it and staff it so that it can work.

HANSEN: The other question is, now that HUD is working on a Housing Allowance concept, and since new communities are basically a new construction oriented kind of venture, suppose Congress decides that Housing Allowances across the country are the answer? If the new communities program is discarded, how would this affect new community development?

MIELDS: I don't really know. I don't believe, however, that we're going to abandon conventional approaches, and I think the interest subsidy programs will be continued is some form. I'm not sure to what extent the Administration will try to expand the Housing

Allowance program. I hope that it will in terms of the experimental programs that are now underway. I don't know how much money they have, but I hope that they will make some money available to an existing new town, that is, a Title VII new town, to see whether or not the community association or public developer could make use of allowances in order to achieve the balanced housing goal. I think new towns in particular would be equipped to deal with housing allowances on a much more comprehensive and useful basis than might be the case in a conventional community.

But I would like to point out—and I have another speech for this—that the thrust of the new communities legislation as it relates to urban revitalization and renewal was designed by Congress to work in the inner city. Of course, we have some problems with the Administration on this, since it seems that most of its political appointees haven't read that part of the act. Eventually we expect the program to work as well in the inner city for new-towns-in-town as we know it works in satellite and free-standing new towns. But I'm really for housing allowances being tried in new towns. I think it could work well.

LARSEN: I work in New York but I live in New Jersey, and I notice that your firm has been the consultant to the City of Paterson. Touching upon the remarks you've made (and the other speech you'd like to give when somebody gets around to reading that aspect of the legislation), in a state like New Jersey, unless there is some hope for the urban aspect of the act, there is probably little hope for the act being effective. It is in that category that I'd like to have you say just a bit more about your hopes for inner city development under the present act or under any future amendments. Further, how hopeful are you?

MIELDS: Well, we have hopes that the Better Communities legislation, which has been introduced to the Congress and is currently pending before the two Banking Committees, and which will not be acted upon until the housing recommendations of the Administration are sent up, will provide special revenue sharing funds for cities. The objectives are very broadly stated and I think will continue to be broadly stated in the legislation. This should make it possible for local governments to exercise a lot more freedom in utilizing grant funds. Hopefully, they will look to what's happening, say, in Cedar-Riverside, Minneapolis; and some of the work that's being done in Jamaica, Queens. Next I hope they will move their program up another step and maybe get down to see Ted (Lamont)—I know they've been down on one or two occasions. Welfare Island is another such community. Chicago is interested in doing some very large-scale development, and perhaps they'll do some under Title VII.

I think the availability of more flexible money could help a great deal. When Title VII was passed there was a Part D that specifically said that grant money could be used to write down land to private developers who undertake inner city developments. However, we could never get Secretary Romney to actually read that part of the act. I believe we once got him to read it, and absorb it, but he didn't believe it. Congress has admonished the Administration on this point. But apparently nobody in this Administration reads congressional reports, including the Office of Management and Budget. In all honesty, however, I do know that HUD reads them.

It's simply a matter of getting people to develop large-scale programs that are comprehensive and really work toward the creation of a community, then to get them to HUD, and finally to get their Congressmen to contact the Administration and influential Republicans to try to get them to accept the new-town-in-town concept.

I don't know of any other way of putting it. But I do know that there are plenty of cities that have the competence and desire and resources necessary to put these things together. Some more planning money would be very helpful, but I do think that the new-town-in-town concept will eventually prevail. You can't accomplish lasting revitalization of inner cities any other way.

CHAPTER

5

SATELLITE COMMUNITIES: TOWARD A RATIONAL GROWTH POLICY

Bernard Weissbourd

I was especially glad this morning to hear Mr. McKissick in the role of developer talk about sewer, water, electricity, bond issues, and money, since I think that gives me license to talk about spirit, which I intend to do later. Mr. McKissick also reminded me of the manager of Harlow, a British new town some 20 miles from London that was started 20 years ago, has 80,000 now living in it and will eventually expand to 120,000. It is a government developed and built project, and referred to by its detractors as a socialist institution.

The manager of Harlow was like any other developer. He was proud that Harlow showed a profit and was able to finance its own expansion, proud that he had succeeded in bringing in industry, and proud that 90 percent of the people who lived there could work there, thus making Harlow a job-linked-housing enterprise. He was also proud of the fact that Harlow had been built before the East End of London was cleared, so that when it came time to clear the East End there was some place for the people to go. England didn't suffer from the kinds of problems we have had in our renewal programs, when we have often operated at cross purposes.

I asked the manager of Harlow the question that is the question of this particular conference. "What about poor people?"

He answered, "When poor people come to Harlow, we have a job for them. When we have a job for them, they are not poor anymore."

I asked, "What about people that are unemployed?"

"That isn't a housing problem," he replied.

His answer, perhaps, poses the question before us here—we need to agree on what we mean by lower income people. I believe that new communities have to provide housing for anyone who works in them. Many industrial workers make $6,000 a year, which is well below medium income. The question regarding people who earn less than that is the question I'd like to hear your answers to at this discussion today.

Now, I do want to talk about money before I talk about spirit because I think money is central to new community programs. I always like to start out talking about money by reminding my hearers that according to John Maynard Keynes compound interest is mankind's great invention. Cash flow is the opposite of compound interest. The dollar I will actually receive twenty years from now is worth only six cents today if I can earn 15 percent of my money. This kind of cash flow or income stream is a significant factor in any business, but particularly in new community development, where the question of future revenues from long-term transactions is crucial. In order to clarify this concept you might try calculating whether or not the Indians made such a bad deal when they sold Manhattan Island for $24. If they had had the opportunity to invest that $24 with 300 years of compound interest the amount that investment would be worth today might conceivably exceed the undeveloped land value of Manhattan Island: $24 compounded for 300 years at 6 percent interest would be worth $935 million today; at 8 percent it would be $250 billion; and at 10 percent it would be $63 trillion. At 15 percent it would be 3.8×10^{19}, or nineteen zeros.

Of course, no planned development takes 300 years to complete. A time line of 15 years is not unusual, however, and even during the 15-year period the difference between what a million dollars would earn at 6 percent and at 15 percent is in excess of 5.7 million dollars. Therefore a private developer borrowing money at the rate of, let's say, 8-10 percent—the current rates today—is not unrealistic in expecting a 15 percent return on his money. For a government developer, however, a lower return is acceptable. British new towns have been earning 8 percent on their investment, which is a very respectable return for a government, because they in turn borrow at 4-5 percent interest. A private developer borrowing at 10 percent and earning 8 percent is operating at a loss. This is one reason I have always taken the position that the government, whether state, local, or federal, must take control of the land for a new town program.

Now, there are lots of implications to this position. For one thing, the government might make money on the land, since urban land values in the United States have been on the increase. They increased more than 400 percent between 1950 and 1970. The single family lot that sold for $1,000 in 1950 cost over $5,000 in 1970. This increase is greater by far than the cost of living in general, and greater even than the increase in building costs. Properly located land is a unique form of monopoly: the supply is limited, and it is the government itself that creates the demand that sends prices soaring, since it is the government that finances the sewers, the water, and the roads that give the land value. I am convinced that a government land program, combined with control over the roads and utilities, would be profitable in the long run.

I want to talk now about something more delicate. I have been talking about the money cost of the growth unit as compared with unplanned development, and now I want to get into the social aspects. Here we run into what seems to be a battle between the environmentalists and the people who are committed to the city, as I am. I think it's very important that we reconcile the environmental aspects of the growth of metropolitan areas with the needs of the poor and with the needs of the city for better housing, better health care, and all the other services needed for the growth of healthy individuals. This really requires a kind of social as opposed to economic cost benefit analysis. For example, how do we discount the future revenues gained from reductions in expenditures to combat crime if, in fact, a new town program helps with this problem? What about the revenues that would have been needed to treat mental illness caused by urban pressures? What about other highly significant cost factors, such as welfare? How do we calculate the exact effect of a new communities program on these problems? At what rate shall we discount cash flow benefits to be derived from desegregation, free choice of residential occupancy, the decrease in air pollution from reduced automobile traffic, and the other advantages of a new community? In other words, how do we do this kind of cost benefit analysis?

A recent Minneapolis/St. Paul transportation study calculated that switching from the automobile to mass transit would save the commuters $872 a year. This was a pretty good report because it noted that reducing highway fatalities, reducing air pollution, improving environmental quality, and providing better access to jobs through rapid transit are also benefits. But it didn't count these benefits—it noted them, but its conclusions weren't based on these points. We have to learn to count social costs and benefits as well as economic ones. The study did not consider what in my mind is the most important factor, and that is what I want to talk about next, namely, how we can pay the entire cost of a new communities program.

Every morning there are two streams of traffic in every metropolitan area. One of them contains inner city residents moving out to suburban jobs; the other contains suburban residents coming in to city jobs. If the cost of those two streams of traffic can be substantially reduced—and I hope to prove that it can—that will more than pay for the entire new communities program. I once had an associate during the Cold War days who really believed that the cost of commuting in this country was so excessive that we might because of it lose the Cold War to Russia. Fortunately for us the Russians may soon be exposed to the same brand of madness. A new plant outside Moscow is producing some 3,000 cars a day, even though there are only nine filling stations in the Moscow metropolitan area. With the introduction of the automobile (they already have the refrigerator) it's likely that the shopping center is not far behind.

Too much of what is being said about the energy crisis is alarmist in character. The oil in the world is disappearing and is becoming excessively expensive to get, but we can make gasoline out of coal as the Germans did in World War II. There is a plant in South Africa that already manufactures gasoline out of coal. The costs of this process are high, but that isn't so alarming because the gross national product seems to double every 15 years. If we have to look forward to gasoline costing twice as much, ultimately it will come to the same percentage of the gross national product. There will, of course, be some side effects when gasoline costs twice what it costs today. For instance, smaller cars, which get 25 to 30 miles per gallon, will be favored. What we should be doing is planning for this situation now, so as to eliminate our dependence on foreign oil.

I firmly believe that the savings in gasoline and automobile transportation costs resulting from a job-linked-housing program, even at present prices, will more than pay for the kind of program we are talking about. A few numbers should illustrate this: there were more than 80 million passenger cars in use in the United States in 1970; in 1969 passenger cars consumed 62 billion gallons of gasoline at a cost of approximately $24 billion. The total cost of operating the 80 million passenger cars in 1970, including depreciation, insurance and repairs, amounted to over $90 billion—more than the U.S. defense budget. This does not include trucks. If we could avoid this double commute (one person to a car every morning) by permitting people to live close to where they work, this would mean a savings of 4.5 billion dollars a year, or 5 percent of our total cost of operating cars. That is more than enough to pay the cost of a new communities program.

I think the energy crisis is really going to move us toward new communities programs; the other factor that will move us in that direction is the abandonment of our cities. This process does not strike at random, nor does it attack only the worst of the housing stock; it is more like a cancer that begins in the heart of a neighborhood, usually a poor minority ghetto, and moves outward to engulf formerly middle-class areas, the inhabitants of which have recently fled as if from a natural disaster.

There are many causes for abandonment, and I don't think I should take the time to go into that complicated process, which ultimately leads to the lenders red-lining the area and disinvesting. To repeat the history of this country's growth in the last twenty-five years would not be worth our time now, but we should note that although the mix of problems is a little different in every city one factor is always crucial: what is not generally understood about the process of abandonment is that it is closely related to the supply and demand of housing for black people. Between 1960 and 1970 the white population of Chicago declined by approximately 550,000, while the black population increased by slightly over 300,000. Other cities with a similar environmental problem exhibit the same phenomenon of white exodus exceeding black influx: Detroit, with 350,000 less whites compared with 180,000 more blacks; St. Louis, with comparable figures of 170,000 and 40,000; and Philadelphia, with 190,000 and 125,000. The list could go on to include Boston, Baltimore, Cleveland, Cincinnati; all display the same disproportion of white exodus in relation to black increase.

This disproportion has brought on a chain reaction that has brought us to the brink of a national disaster. Since there is no place for the people from the ghetto to go except an adjoining neighborhood they spread in that direction, leaving a vacuum at the center from which they move. Middle-class black people can move into vacated housing in formerly all-white or mixed neighborhoods, but the poor get left behind. Since not enough money comes in to maintain them, whole neighborhoods are abandoned, the good housing along with the bad.

I don't want to give the false impression that there is now a surplus of housing for black people. We also have to look at the demand side of the equation. For years the blacks in a city like Chicago have been impacted in a geographical area too small for their numbers. Vacant housing may exist in other sections of the city, but it has not been available to blacks; a reasonable vacancy rate exists side by side with extreme overcrowding. Although some middle-class blacks have been able to buy their way out of the ghetto by paying more than the housing is worth in adjacent areas, the poor are left behind with few housing alternatives. They don't have the money either to rent or buy the available housing at market rates except by doubling up and therefore are compelled to live in overcrowded conditions. The landlord is equally handicapped: he has nowhere to unload his building.

I know we are supposed to be talking about new towns, but to me new towns cannot be considered independently of the central cities. Unless the new town becomes one of the instruments for relieving the ghettoization of America and becomes an instrument of desegregation, it is not accomplishing its most important goal. At the same time, as a nation we have yet to give serious consideration to the task of housing the very poorest part of our population. We tend to treat poverty as if it were a temporary condition and rather like the flu; yet there are and will continue to be many people who simply do not have any bootstraps by which to pull themselves up. We need to develop a national strategy that will permit the poor to live in dignity and, hopefully, provide their children with the opportunity to escape the poverty cycle, which frequently perpetuates itself generation after generation.

I, for one, strongly recommend that the housing allowance program be part of the new town strategy, because the housing allowance puts money into the hands of poor people. If you ask poor people what they need they answer, money. Among other choices, money can help the poor improve their earning ability. The problem of new towns for poor people is that the housing is all new, and being all new it's all expensive. We have to provide the option of new towns too, but we very much need to be able to permit a large family to buy a single family home in the inner city in which to raise children, instead of forcing every lower income city family to live in a high-rise public housing project. Other options for ghetto residents must be provided in order to relieve the pressure on the adjoining neighborhoods, thereby bringing a halt to the process that leads to abandonment of the inner cities. I suggest that we cannot afford to abandon our cities.

In conclusion, I want to call your attention to the report of the National Policy Task Force of the American Institute of Architects (AA) on a plan for urban growth. This document has become the center of a thrust toward desegregated new town development based on government financed land, to place these new towns where we need them and where they would do the most good as a desegregation strategy.

At the AA Convention, which occurred earlier this month, the general consensus was that the constraints for the adoption of a rational, purposeful program that would accomplish the goals for all of us assembled here, were constraints of the spirit. That, somehow, we in America were hung up with a spirit that doesn't work for modern times. We have to approach our problem with a more mature spirit, however, and realize that we have to do with what we have, where we have to deal with all of the population. We have to be mature Americans.

Discussion

ERICKSON: I'm working out of Washington. I picked up your comment about the federal, state, and local government owning land in these new towns. I am very much in favor of the community owning and developing such resources as shopping centers, which produce revenue from which the lower income people can benefit. However, I am not convinced as yet that the new community is going to deal with low income housing simply because HUD tells the developer that he has to put in 28 percent of his units for lower income housing. What really concerns me is that poor and lower income people will be living in new communities that, I think, are geared for middle-class living, although there may be some spin-off. Maybe we can learn from technology how to build low income housing, but I don't see new towns as a viable option or viable answer to meeting the needs of low-income housing. But if the communities could own land. . . .

WEISSBOURD: I think we're in great danger of seeking perfection, of throwing out the baby with the bath water. When I say that I think the government ought to own land, I mean that maybe the federal government would have to finance state and local government ownership of the land in a sort of a 90/10 grant program, such as we used for the highway system, for the purpose of assembling land in the places where the new communities will do the most good. The new communities can serve several purposes, but those that most directly affect inner city problems are those on the outskirts of metropolitan areas. Many such areas don't have land available. This morning a man from New Jersey pointed out the difficulty of assembling land for that purpose in New Jersey. Yet if you had power of eminent domain you could do it. For instance, there are places in New Jersey where there is enough good land but the ownership is spread out.

Here is where I think government ownership of land comes in. The urban renewal program is a model here because under it the government can impose public control over certain pieces in new communities and then sell off land to builders to develop neighborhoods. Unlike urban renewal, however, it should not have to be a write-down. In fact it may be a write-up, a profit to the government. As to the question of economic integration, I suggest you not be too pessimistic. There is even now some sympathy in the suburbs for the idea that firemen, teachers, and other suburban employees should be allowed to live in the towns that employ them. This holds especially for towns that are dependent on industry for their tax base. A program that insists that people who work in a plant be given the right to live close by will accomplish a great deal, and you may find the government enforcing this concept. I also suggest that if you can house people earning $6,000 a year and up you've accounted for 80 percent of the population. The other 20 percent is, of course, a difficult and perplexing problem.

CHAPTER 6

THE IMPACT OF JOB-LINKED-HOUSING ON LABOR AND NEW COMMUNITIES
Gus Tyler

I would like to set Job-Linked-Housing against a larger background, namely, the allocation of people. In this last presidential campaign there was considerable discussion of the problem of the redistribution of wealth in the United States, and I gather that problem may be with us for some years. I would like to suggest as a major priority of the United States a redistribution of the people in terms of where they live. One of the common clichés of our day is the need to reorder priorities; I would place at the top of the agenda this redistribution of one of our most misallocated natural resources, namely, the people themselves.

I think that we are presently entrapped in a dangerous misallocation of population. It was not planned by any evil genius; it came about through the accidents of history and time. Our society may at the present time be the victim of the socioeconomic byproduct of other major trends as well. We have dangerously dense populations that are misplaced in terms of job needs and in terms of the expected amenities of a civilization.

This is not really the first time in history that we have run up against a problem like this, but it seems to me that our most immediate problem stems from the post-World War II period, when a major, rapid, and I would suggest an almost catastrophic shift of populations in the United States took place. The problem arises out of the size and velocity of that shift, which has left us rather dazed in terms of finding necessary social accommodations, and also out of its irrationality, in terms of where people live and where they have to make a living.

Gus Tyler had planned to address the conference. His prepared speech is included for the record.

Although the focus of this problem is the city, I would suggest that the problem really begins in rural America. New policies were pursued by this country for several decades. One was to increase productivity of the land, and this we were to accomplish by all kinds of scientific inventions. We were vastly successful and could make eight stalks grow where one grew before. American agricultural production overwhelmed this nation and the world as well.

The second policy we pursued was to maintain the market by encouraging restriction of production by legislation that rewarded people for nonproduction.

We therefore had two contradictory policies going at once: increased productivity and curtailed production. The result of all of this was to render several million people in the United States obsolete. In the past these people had made their living from the soil or lived in small rural towns. This meant that about one million people a year were dispossessed from agricultural America and propelled into our industrial society in the post-World War II period. It was a massive and overwhelming wave. In twenty years some 20 million people were driven from the soil to the city.

Throughout history, whenever a wave of immigration of such dimension has taken place it has brought on a cultural clash that manifested itself in crime, disorder, riots, hatred, violence, and explosion.

The demographers refer to this population shift as "rural push" and "urban pull." It sets in motion a second dynamic, "urban push" and "suburban pull," or population movement out of the city and into the suburbs. A kind of dual society is now created in which all those, or most of those, who could escape from the city, escaped.

This was not simply a movement of residences, but also a movement of jobs, because the inner city became an increasingly uncomfortable place to continue industrial production. The taxes were prohibitively high and the services were relatively less. Land was extremely costly, and therefore the only way to expand industrial production in the city was to move it vertically. But vertical movement is terribly expensive. In addition, the movement of goods, raw materials in and finished material out, is increasingly difficult in the inner city because of its traffic problems.

Finally, the city, as its costs mount and its debts mount with them, is driven to try to meet its bills by raising taxes. The inner city, therefore, becomes a difficult place to continue even the same production that may have been going on for 50 years or more. Hence the urban push-suburban pull applies not simply to persons shifting their homes to a bit of greenery; it also applies to manufacturing and other branches of our economy shifting their locus out of the cities into the suburbs and, if you please, into the exurbs.

Many manufacturing establishments, especially in the inner cities, were and still are engaged in light manufacture, which in the United States is pretty much labor intensive production. Labor intensive production inevitably reaches out to the marginal populations, whether they are racially a minority or just poor.

In the United States, at least since the 1890s, light manufacture in the central cities has been the first rung on the ladder of economic upward mobility. The way people moved into the economic system was by moving into light manufacture with its rather simplified handwork. The ability to make a living at that level also enabled marginal populations to begin the gradual process of acculturation to an urban society. This pattern of the past has been disrupted, as marginal populations move into the inner cities, and the jobs they normally drifted into move to the outer fringes of the city, the inner suburbs, the suburbs, and the exurbs. In terms of manufacture we have unwittingly created an almost perfect mismatch of populations and jobs, a mismatch for which we are now paying a huge price in the United States in terms of our welfare bill and an even greater price in terms of our mounting fears about the jungle in the city.

A second kind of mismatch is also developing; as populations and employers leave the city, decay, ruin, abandonment, rats, and the weather take over the buildings. Sometimes riots also add to the destruction, and sometimes so does urban renewal. After the rot, something else comes. After the rot comes the bulldozer cleaning it out; and then gorgeous office buildings, corporate headquarters, museums, theaters, centers of art, and professional offices begin to take over much of the inner city, offering jobs, primarily white collar jobs, to the more affluent, who at this moment, are probably not living in the inner city, nor near the inner city, nor even in the middle belt of the city. They too are mismatched, because daily they have to make the journey from the outer to the inner. While some of the poor people of the inner city reach out to the outer manufacturing jobs, in most cases they are unable to afford this move and are left to their own rather disastrous devices.

As a result the work week is not really 40 hours at all, because the people must get into their automobiles and drive to work an hour to an hour and a half. This misallocation of residences and jobs is, in this sense, destroying one of the great advances of our society, the democratization of leisure.

To move from home to job we depend very heavily on the automobile. The automobile, which is supposed to provide mobility, is increasingly the perfect example of immobility. It can sit in midtown Manhattan for five or ten minutes and move one block. Everywhere in the country great highways are referred to as the largest parking lots in the world. The automobile has poisoned our atmosphere and gobbled up our income. Property that could yield taxes and many other things is being paved over and converted into roads and parking lots.

I want to make two more points about this general need for a reallocation of populations. The first concerns the female labor force in the United States. At most such conferences we tend, I do not know why, to view our economic problem out of a past from which we have not yet been properly liberated. May I point out that at the present time forty percent of the labor force in the United States is female. Forty percent! Not so long ago it was thirty percent. I'll make a simple projection: by 1980 about fifty percent of the labor in the United States will be female.

My second point stems from the first. Forty-three percent of the mothers in the United States hold jobs away from home. This includes half of the mothers with children between 6 and 18, a third of the mothers with children under 6, and a quarter of the mothers with children under 3. Please make no moral judgment; these are not unloving mothers, eager to dump their kids. The evidence is that in 90 percent of the cases they are loving mothers, who want to make enough money to enable the family to live better, in a better neighborhood. The truth is that it's the mothers of the United States who have waged the war against poverty.

There is, however, a problem: although the average family income goes up somewhat because of the woman at work, what happens to the kids? It's a mounting problem in the United States, a problem that affects some 7 million children and may be affecting them in a crippling kind of way.

Mothers have sought solutions. Neighborhood care is inadequate and the mother is far away. Many employers have tried to encourage job-linked-nurseries, but they have almost uniformly failed because the mother has to travel with the child by mass transit or car for 30 minutes to an hour to the place of work, and go through the same thing again at the end of the day. Because of this, after an initial burst of enthusiasm many of the mothers gave up the idea. Rationally, the best approach is to make residences more reasonably within striking distance of the job; this would ease our mounting problem of child care. I'm not saying the problem would be solved, but certainly it would be eased if employers and communities could move toward providing day-care facilities, full time or part time, for the children of this growing army of working mothers.

I assume one emphasis at this conference is on locating residences near existing employment facilities. I would like to suggest that at some point we ought to be reaching out for a larger concept, in which we move both employment and housing simultaneously in a rational way. At the present time I am advised that, as a result of the rural push-urban pull, 75 to 80 percent of the American population sits on something like 1.5 percent of the land area of the United States. This is a totally irrational kind of density. It has developed through three accidents of history, the first of which is the accident that 18th-century cities located at the crossing of waterways. The second is the accident that 19th century cities developed at the crossing of railways. The third, and 20th century, accident is the displacement of 20 million people out of rural America into urban America. Nobody planned any of this, but here we are choking with it. We have this crazy density in the cities while half of the counties in the United States have lost population in the last 20 years, leaving ghost towns, poor towns, and decaying towns. Rural and small town poverty in the United States are frightening to behold and utterly inexcusable.

There are those who are thinking of expanding job-linked-housing to include 200 new communities in the United States. This would be a redistribution or reallocation, both of populations and of employment opportunities. It could do a great deal for the nation by easing the unnerving congestion of the cities. Undoubtedly, racial and ethnic tensions would continue for a long time; they have already been on the face of the earth for several thousand years. It's easier to live with tensions when you have some elbow room and do not have to step on top of one another, however. A massive job-linked-housing program could mean full employment for the United States from now to the year 2000. It could provide a rational answer to the ecological problem of the cities, which serve as the focal point of poison for a whole society.

Job-linked-housing could ultimately be tied in with an expanded concept of society in which we increasingly plan in a rational way for convenience of residence to work.

CHAPTER

7

RESPONSE PANEL
Glenn Claytor
Maria Perez
Cushing N. Dolbeare
Robert E. Simon, Jr.

CLAYTOR: The National Urban League, along with a number of my colleagues at the NAACP and elsewhere, is concerned with new communities as a possible relief for some of the problems in housing for minorities and low income families. A considerable amount of discussion has focused on this in the past year, and in the National Urban League we have formed a subcommittee of our National Housing Committee to deal with the problems of new communities. This is an indication of our desire to have a voice in social planning and perhaps even become principals in the development of a new town.

Many issues have been brought up at this meeting that I may not be able to deal with in depth, but that are close to my heart. For instance, there has been considerable discussion at the Urban League about a national land use policy. We have written extensively on this subject and have testified before Congress; it's certainly not a new thought. I can remember reading Herbert Franklin on national land use eight years ago when he was at Syracuse University, and I consider myself a student of his in that regard. Also, I have developed some ideas of my own about national land use, including a belief that we should move toward a land use policy that deals with land as a public resource. God knows we have already had land use policies: the first one was to take the land from the Indians; the second was the Louisiana Purchase, then Alaska, and so on. The Homestead Act and the taking of land for our railroads are also examples of our land use policies. We're very strong on the notion that we ought to take land in sufficient quantities, acquire it in advance of need, and then apply it in a rational fashion to facilitate orderly growth.

Some of the speakers I heard this morning have left me somewhat nonplused. I couldn't understand Ted Lamont's arithmetic: in terms of the impact of the construction of homes in new communities, we should keep in mind that at any given time when we talk about new construction we are probably talking about less than 5 percent of the housing available to anyone, rich or poor, white or black. The existing housing stock is above 80 million units, and that should really be our main concern. Many here have spoken about that with respect to the problem of abandonment. Housing abandonment puts me to thinking of pouring water into a bucket that has a hole in the bottom: while we talk of producing half a million units for low income housing, we are probably losing in excess of that amount through abandonment. Last year in New York City some estimates put the loss of housing through abandonment at over 40,000 units. Our survey completed two years ago for seven major cities indicated a loss of over 100,000 in just those cities alone. HUD was given 20 million dollars to do research and demonstrations, but in the last year and a half it has done nothing except in the Crown Heights Brooklyn area, and I believe that attempt was unsuccessful.

Let me deal for a moment with new communities as they affect minorities. We at the National Urban League believe that an appropriate way to relieve the pressure from the inner cities is to increase peoples' options. We always say that the question is not one of integration versus separation, but rather of increasing the options available to minority persons. We hold to that.

Some of the things I heard this morning that I liked came from Floyd McKissick, a man I've always loved. Soul City was very generous in showing us and the NAACP people around. What I liked especially about Soul City was that it dealt with economic development as a salutary offshoot of housing activity. There is no more basic activity in America. Last year 100 billion dollars plus was spent for residential construction alone, yet minorities got less than .5 billion, about .5 percent. I think it is an opportunity for turning defeat into victory by bringing blacks along in the economic development aspect of housing as well as in the shelter aspect of it.

Some things I heard from my HUD friends, Ted Lamont and Peggy Wireman, whom I respect, are still rather tentative; "We will encourage. . . . We will promote. . . ."

Alex Greendale, next time we get together, whether it be under the auspices of this group or another, we should have more developers present. It seems to me that we really haven't put them through the test. I've heard them speak impressively about their social conscience and their desire to do social planning, but as I view it from my side of the fence it looks to me like business as usual. It's old wine in new bottles: I've been to more than half of the 15 new communities that are funded, and those that I visited (and I have friends that go back ten years or more in places like Riverton and Gananda) have really no black presence at all. I mean not only not in policy-making positions; some of these new towns don't even have black secretaries. Yet they come to these conferences and they talk about social planning.

As I see it there is no evidence, nor any great pressure from HUD, to encourage social planning as it affects our minorities. The developers could evidence their concern by utilizing the social planning capabilities of such groups as the NAACP and the Urban League. I feel HUD needs to do more in that direction. The Urban League recently joined the League of New Community Developers and began to formulate a package for new community developers, indicating our capability in this area. I think this is one time the minorities cannot afford to wake up too late. My figures indicate there will be some 80 million additional Americans by the year 2000: that's some 30 million household formations. Meanwhile, HUD talks about only .9 million units to be produced in new communities; there should be a better response to the magnitude of the problem.

PEREZ: My concern is mostly with what I didn't hear. Everything I heard sounded rosy: "We will be part of the program . . . we will have X percentage of units . . . and so forth." But where is our minority input? How can we really enjoy that percentage? Let's come down to earth and look at the facts. Can we share in the planning of new cities? I think it is a new opportunity. It is a must. But I also think that plans are only as good as the planners and whoever implements what the planners plan. If we are not being included in the planning process, then there is no way you can judge if it is of benefit to the minority population.

I saw very little concern here with how to utilize the expertise of the minorities. I believe the minorities have something to offer; we have matured and we know what we want. We know that we cannot live in a segregated world. We know that by utilizing our resources in a constructive fashion we can help develop new communities that will benefit all people. There will be times when planners and minorities will disagree as well as agree, but what is essential is that we plan together.

I also believe, and strongly, that new towns by themselves are not going to solve the problem unless they contain provisions for all the needs people have in health, recreation, religion, and every other aspect of life, to give them an opportunity to grow and become part of a total environment. What I would really like to see is an opportunity for minority groups to make their contribution to the new town movement. We have something to offer. We know what we need, we know what all the people need, and we also know that in order to survive we must all work together. We at this conference should and could grow together, but in order to do so we must solve a big problem that has to be dealt with first by everyone; namely, attitude. Those on both sides of the fence must do much to change their attitudes; to begin to understand each others' problems; and at the same time not to interfere with each others' growth, work, and development in the new town.

DOLBEARE: I agree with most of what Glenn Claytor and Maria Perez have said, but I'm going to be sharply critical, more critical than I'd be if I had more than five minutes. Rather than presenting a balanced perspective, I want to try to inject some balance into today's program.

We have talked about constraints of the spirit, but it seems to me that there are basic constraints in addition to those of the spirit in the institutions that we're dealing with, to which we're looking for the development of new towns. The basic questions should deal with the kind of institutions we want and who should control them. Are we really going to consider the provision of decent housing for poor people and minority people to be a public responsibility in which these people have something to say? We need to ask ourselves what kind of institutions we really want to carry out housing development in this country and whether we can use new towns to create and support those institutions.

The National Tenants Organization is basically an organization of victims: minority people, poor people, blacks, Latinos, and native Americans. These people have been excluded from the decision-making process in housing and from participation in decent housing. Except in Soul City, they are being excluded from any kind of voice in the planning or building of new towns.

We recognized this morning that housing patterns have been a basic cause of polarization in this country, and we've looked at new towns as a possible opportunity for a solution. But we've looked at new towns as an opportunity for a solution without involving half of the people who have been polarized.

We talked about scale, and the rough calculations I did when the question was asked about the scale of new towns under the HUD program indicates that it will be about 3 percent of the housing production between now and the year 2000. If one-third of that is subsidized, and that's generous since we have the figure at 28 percent, that's 1 percent of total production between now and the year 2000. That's a pretty small drop in the bucket, it seems to me.

We heard a lot of code words this morning, or at least to me they sounded like code words. "Revitalization of our cities" was one. Revitalization of our cities sounds like the 1973 equivalent of urban renewal. I haven't yet seen a mechanism for revitalizing our cities that didn't add up to displacing poor and minority people and trying to lure more affluent, majority people back so as to provide a "broader economic base."

We talked about the evil of the concentration of low income families—the social disorganization. What we're really talking about are concentrations of people who have been excluded from participation in the economic, social, and political aspects of American society. If we would make their participation possible, however, I don't think we would have to be quite so concerned about the concentration of low income families.

We talked about "balanced suburban communities." Only one-third of new housing production is subsidized, in a society where three-fourths of our households cannot afford unsubsidized new housing. To me "balanced communities" seems to be a code for too little and too late racial and economic integration.

It's a basic question, it seems to me, of who is going to decide the patterns of development. What should be the federal role? Hugh Mields had a lot of federal policy statements this morning, but he omitted the one in the 1949 Housing Act that declared it to be national policy to provide every American family with a decent home and a suitable living environment. Recently Secretary Lynn asked organizations for their comments on the role of the federal government in housing. The National Tenants Organization suggested that the basic question we need to decide is whether to reaffirm that statement of federal housing policy or repeal it. If we are going to abandon an effective federal role in housing we ought to repeal it.

We talked about a definition of low income. There are 4 million tenant families in this country with incomes below $2,000 a year, but there are only 1 million housing units that rent at rents that fall within 25 percent of their income. That leaves a gap of 3 million units at the very bottom of the income scale. That gap wasn't discussed this morning, since we talked about people who were working. People with incomes below $2,000 a year either aren't working or they're not getting paid.

The question before us today is, "Are New Towns for Low Income People?" As these programs are developed so far they may provide shelter for some low income people, but as I heard it this morning they don't provide for participation. "Is there a need for a network of organizations to concern themselves with new towns?" Well, there is, but it seems to me that it needs to be broader than that. What there needs to be is a network of organizations concerned with the housing needs of people who are presently excluded, although perhaps less in new towns than elsewhere, from getting decent housing in a suitable living environment.

SIMON: I'm following three advocacy planners to this microphone, but I am not one of them. I am where I like to be and where I believe the real world is. I would strongly suggest that advocacy planners be very careful not to swap the best thing going at this time. I am not an expert in the politics of advocacy planning and advocacy promoting, but it sure as hell seems to me that if there is something good going, and if it doesn't represent everything that you could possibly imagine or dream, and if it is run by human beings (which is about all we've got to run things with now), then the advocacy planners should do a couple of things: (1) get their facts straight—I think that's quite important—and (2) in their editorial department, at least, support the best that's available.

As far as getting facts straight, let me say that in addition to having been involved in Reston, I am the developer of Riverton. Riverton was cited totally incorrectly, and the government was also cited incorrectly as regards its black program. One of the things that we pride ourselves on is our black recruiting program at the executive level, the professional level as well as the secretarial level. I would like to have our advocates come to Riverton and learn the facts. Our entire organization is involved in this recruiting effort, and regardless of how I might feel about it it would not be if it weren't for the constraints put on us by the federal government.

I want to say in passing that I don't like references to drops in the bucket when we are talking about as many as 5 million people. From my point of view, if you do something for a million people that's fantastic. Drops in the bucket to the contrary, one way of looking at 1 to 5 million people is to say, That's for 1 to 5 million people! That's pretty exciting!

Now, in the excitement department, the big thrill for me today was listening to Floyd McKissick, because he has had the toughest job of any of us and it looks like he's going to have the most exciting project. I congratulated him privately, and now I do it publicly.

I'd like to get back to this government thing, because the prevailing sounds from those who preceded me is that the new towns program is all so vague and unenforceable. The lawyers in this room know what default means. Default means that you've lost your project. If the government wants to it can take over your project, and it's been made easy for the government to do just that. There is a thing we call a "joker's share of stock." Uncle Sam has that, and that share can run the whole show if the developer is in default. The project agreement is a very specific agreement. We signed one, and so did all the other fourteen developers. In our agreement we say that if there is federal subsidy we will see that we get it, and that we will deliver 40 percent in low to moderate income housing. It also says that if there is no federal subsidy we will subsidize land to a specific extent.

The formula is complicated and I don't even have it in my head now, but it's not insubstantial. It's nowhere comparable to 40 percent.

If there are federal subsidies available, as we have heard this morning that there probably would be for new communities, and if Riverton doesn't make any application, and if Riverton does not have blacks on its staff, and did not have minorities in the construction crews and on the sites, the federal government is empowered to take over the project. You can't set up anything stronger than that! The developer's performance is the easiest thing in the world to measure: for every 100 houses, how many are under 235 and 236? This is no mystery at all; it's easy. It will be obvious if you are not on target, and if you're not the government can come in and take over your project.

Now, I agree with anyone in this room who asks, "How is the government going to monitor these projects?" The government has a very difficult job, and it's still in the future because all of these Title VII projects are new. But the mechanism has been set up, and the advocacy people should watch how the government performs. This is a very excellent program that has been set up, and it is the first program in the history of the United States that has mandated community planning as well as housing construction.

I assure you that there have been millions and millions of dollars spent on the planning. Am I right, Floyd? Is there a single developer who hasn't spent a hundred thousand dollars on this kind of planning? And $100,000 is low. The question is, what are we going to do with the plans? That's something to monitor, and monitor carefully, but for God's sake don't lose sight of the fact that this is the only place in the United States where this kind of work is going on, mandated by the government. It's not going on in every suburb. It's going on in a few suburbs, maybe, but very few.

I am for the federal land bank suggested by an earlier speaker. There was a land banking program of sorts outside of Stockholm in the 1920s with which you may be familiar. The Swedes bought all the land around Stockholm, because they thought that one day the city might expand and they would need it. It came in handy. I think that's a fine device that we should push for.

A federal land bank for any other land concept will have very little bearing on the cost of housing. That is something that seemed to be quite confusing this morning. What land banking will do is make available land in chunks that are large enough to allow significant projects to be built when it's timely to build them. However, the raw cost of land is, I believe, under 5 percent of the finished product under any circumstances. Whether or not you make a substantial saving in the cost of raw land, you are still going to have to come up with a costs solution.

I would like to end up with this question: Do all of you think it's worthwhile for us to consider <u>low cost</u> housing nationally? So far everyone has been talking about <u>low income</u> housing, although there is low cost housing in many parts of the world.

There are two reasons why we do not have low cost housing as a major national phenomenon; the first is our design standards. Our design standards for low income housing are far in excess of design standards for middle income housing in Western Europe, let alone Asia. Is this an area in which we should become involved?

The second reason we do not have low cost housing is labor costs. Quite a few, although not all, of the new communities are building under the Davis-Bacon regulations. Davis-Bacon requires that the prevailing wage will be the wage paid. One of the ways of lowering the costs of housing is by self-help housing, which has been experimented with on a small scale in this country. The self-help housing I saw on the Indian reservations was particularly interesting.

It is conceivable that some housing solutions will be found by going back to our earlier days and reviving customs like barn-raising where people get together and build collaboratively. Perhaps this is something that could be done in Soul City; if it could, it might be one of the most important things Soul City could do. Interestingly enough, there has been an experiment on this in Fairfax County, where kids in training to become craftsmen are building houses with the help of professionals; the cost under these circumstances can be substantially lowered. Since this is a conference on housing for low income people, therefore, I wonder if part of it shouldn't be addressed to the possibility of building low cost housing.

Discussion

DeBOER: Now, we want some back and forth here at the table. We've already had some, but we have a limited amount of time so I'll ask you to keep your remarks fairly brief. We will have an opportunity in the small groups discussions that will follow for further comments.

CLAYTOR: Let me say publicly that no intentional slight of Riverton was meant. The name came to mind because I spent some time in the Rochester area. I meant to refer to the class of new communities developers. I do stand by the remarks that I made generally, but I don't want to get into a debate about it. If it was misinterpreted, I apologize.

But leaving aside Robert Simon's gratuitous remark about the real world, I would like to go on to something else; namely his interesting observation that he thinks we "advocacy planners" should somehow be involved in the monitoring. Speaking as a developer he suggested that we should monitor those who are supposed to enforce the regulations developers are supposed to observe. It would have been more interesting if he had told us what he as a developer was going to do, than it was when he told us what we were supposed to do.

Leaving that aside, I want to go quickly to the question of land use. I'd like this group to discuss the way we represent ourselves to our friends in Congress and elsewhere with respect to a more explicit land use plan than we have talked about so far. (I think Ted mentioned that he would "encourage" states to set up structures similar to the New York State Urban Development Corporation.) Perhaps what we need is a national UDC, which would in fact be regionalized. This national UDC would acquire land in advance of need, have binding authority, have the power of eminent domain, and also the power to enforce nationally set production goals.

American history is replete with examples in which the federal government has preempted an area and left it to the state to do or not to do, in their wisdom or in their capacity—or not in their wisdom or not in their capacity—in such areas as welfare and education. Where the states could not find the wherewithal to make the necessary changes, the federal government came in to make them, in keeping with national goals. I think that is what we are going to have to shoot for eventually: I don't think the new communities themselves are going to change things around. I don't think the present form of community development is really going to get us out of the hole we are now in. I think in the final analysis we are going to develop a national scheme for the use of land, and I think we begin to do that by creating an agency that can deal with it.

PEREZ: I want to say to Mr. Simon that there is nothing wrong with being an advocacy planner, because advocacy planners are needed in new towns. What I do feel is needed is a new look at the clauses, in the contracts that are presently given to developers, that refer to minority groups' participation in the planning process of these new cities and their role in decision making. These clauses are very loose and generally subjected to a series of "ifs"; no strict guidelines exist, nor is there a specific directive to monitor implementation effectively. The developer only has to show, if this participation falls short, that an effort directed toward minority participation was made, and this suffices to put him in the clear. Even if the developer does not give the minority groups the opportunity to make suggestions and participate in the decision making process, he will be penalized only if the government so chooses, despite the contract he has signed with the government to honor these clauses.

The result is that the poor, the blacks, and the Spanish-speaking are not involved, nor are they engaged in the total development of new town conceptions. They are forced to accept housing that does not reflect their culture, needs, or desires.

I also feel that this lack of minority involvement creates housing design and construction that may be alien to these minorities, that they do not like or have pride in. Consequently their maintenance of these homes will be poor and in some cases may even go to the extreme of vandalization.

I do not say that new towns will provide housing for every person who needs housing. That is a dream that cannot come true. But new towns can provide, as Mr. Simon says, "sweat equity" housing. If you are going to do that for low income people, however, they must be consulted every step of the way, and involved in a more meaningful way.

The idea of new towns and planning for them is an excellent idea and I support it wholeheartedly, but I want to repeat my fear that we will again fail the minorities by ignoring their wants, desires, and cultures, as well as the positive improvements they can make for all.

Also, I am concerned by the way their participation, input and engagement is defined or presupposed to be defined in the present conception of new cities. No emphasis or recognition is being given to the need to plan, develop, and implement the new town concept in an actively collaborative fashion. I want to bring this problem to the awareness of all parties concerned.

WEISSBOURD: I'm a little troubled about the mood here. Last fall (in 1972) all of us were very discouraged about the housing program, and we had an Administration that never really intended to do anything about it. The new towns program, however, represents a ray of hope. Granted, that it's just a small part of the total housing picture, and it isn't addressing the fundamental housing problems of the metropolitan areas. Some 30 metropolitan areas in the United States have 85 percent of the problem, so that we are talking a little bit in a vacuum. We must come to grips with the total housing market, which includes the entire metropolitan area, and we must move this problem to the metropolitan scale and make decisions that are metropolitan in scope. That's how you really get participation by tenants and poor people in the total planning process.

There is no way for poor people to be involved in new town development. New towns probably won't house them anyway unless they move there to get a job. It is only in the context of the total metropolitan process that we can begin to make sense out of the overall housing market, and when we do we will have to face up to what I believe has been the heart of the problem for the last 20 years, namely, the public housing program, with which we have been trying to house the lowest segment of the income population in new housing and which has antagonized the middle income segment of our population living in old housing. Middle income people feel they have been paying for public housing, and they have developed such resistance to it because it has become segregated housing, in contrast to what public housing was like under Roosevelt.

The middle class was willing to pay for public housing before it became segregated. To change the picture we must understand metropolitan areas. Only then will we be able to plan realistic new living arrangements in new towns and in older housing in the cities. (incidentally, some of this older housing is very good housing.)

With the resurgence of Congress I'm more optimistic that there is a possibility that we may get legislation that would really put such a program on a solid basis. That will require unity, however, and there is some danger that in our discussion here we're being distracted by side issues. I think the central issue, as one speaker said, is national control over the land. This will get the entire program moving.

DeBOER: This kind of dialogue is useful. There's a saying that politics makes strange bedfellows; there's also a saying that politics makes bedfellows strange. I'm hoping that new town politics may make some congenial bedfellows out of people that have varying points of view.

DOLBEARE: I have never thought of myself as a planner, but I'm delighted to have been referred to as an advocate. As an advocate I am constantly being told that I should live in the real world for a change. There are, however, a lot of dimensions to reality. I think Mr. Weissbourd added a very important one just now when he said we really ought to be looking at the total context of the housing picture, especially public housing.

Public housing started in 1937, but has it evolved into having the basic elements that can be molded into a viable program for housing low income people? I think it's very important for us to remember that public housing exists, and that if you have tenant participation on the board, public housing, in new towns and out, is a viable means for developing new housing with participation of low income people. And yet the Administration seems to be abandoning public housing.

Finally, a note on subsidies. Public housing subsidies run to not quite a billion dollars a year, I believe. Total housing subsidies run to 8 billion dollars a year. In 1971, 6 billion dollars of that was in the form of tax subsidies, the expenditures that are deducted from income tax returns, and those go very largely to the middle income families, the families who most resent our housing subsidies for the poor. I think it's important to remember those figures and to publicize them, because most people receiving housing subsidies don't realize they are getting higher subsidies than most low income people.

SIMON: I would like to impress upon all of you what it's like to be a new town developer as compared, say, to being mayor. I really believe that community participation regardless of the structure is much more important to a new town developer than to a mayor, and this is the reason. The mayor gets elected for two or four years or whatever. He says the things he thinks he has to say in order to get elected. After election he does what he wants to do, what the power structures indicate he should do, or what his conscience may dictate, until it's time for the next election. Then if he wants to be reelected he begins talking again. In contrast, the new town developer is faced with his constituency every day. He has to market, and there is no tougher market than a community that is dissatisfied with what has happened. I can assure you that in my years at Reston we listened very closely to what our constituency had to say. If somebody was dissatisfied about something he got attention very quickly. This was not because of our good nature but because of our good business sense. So that's my thought within the time constraint: participatory democracy doesn't only work at the ballot box; it also works in the market place.

DeBOER: At this point we will break up into five groups so that everyone will have an opportunity to have his or her say. Obviously we don't have the time to do that in a group of this size in a plenary session. The purpose of this next period is to discuss this question: "Is there a need for a network of organizations to address the issue of the needs of lower income Americans in new towns?" There will be two parts to this, the first of which is to define, as you talk together, the possible roles for a national network that might be formed and what you think such a network or coalition could be or should be. Remember that a coalition is a coming together of people or organizations that might be quite different in many basic ways but that are united about the particular issue in question.

Second, after you have agreed on what such a network might be like, then discuss what groups and organizations might be interested and in what way they might become part of such a coalition. Part of the discussion, I hope, will include the question, What's the agenda for this kind of a coalition? Should it be to push for the kind of legislation we were talking about here for national land use, an extension of UDC, as has been suggested? Should pressure be put on the Administration, or should input be given to Congress now that someone has said it's getting up on its hind legs again? What should be the kinds of input such a coalition might exert?

CHAPTER

8

PLENARY SESSION

Group 1, ORR: One of the things we discussed in our group was that there seemed to be a proliferation of groups concerned with new towns. Reference was made to the League of New Community Developers and the Association For New Community Social Planning. Are we going to duplicate what these groups are doing? The point was also raised that we seem to be concerned with relating upward. We wondered, if such a coalition was formed, if it might consider relating downward to include the people who live in these new communities. We thought perhaps a regional housing authority could play an advocate's role for those who lived in new towns and even housing development groups. Generally, we agreed that "coalition" is a catchall term, and we thought it should include more than just housing: for example, education, jobs, and social welfare as well.

Finally, we agreed that, yes, it would be good to have a coalition if it would deal with the real issues that affect all of America today. Our focus would be on new communities, and we would hope that the result of such a coalition would be that these new communities could begin to provide solutions on these issues, that in the end the experience that comes out of such coalitions should be transferable to all the 36,000 communities throughout the country. We had one other recommendation, namely, that if such a coalition is formed we should work very hard to make certain that we coordinate our efforts with other groups, such as those I have already mentioned.

Group 2, HAMBLEN: I think our report is essentially the same. Our group discussed the day's proceedings and concluded that

---

The groups met separately for forty-five minutes and then reported back for this session.

individual laissez faire capitalism as we have known it in America cannot successfully develop new towns that would include a substantial number of lower income Americans. There must be a joining together of public and private resources to successfully launch such a venture. Also, we have much experience to fall back on from new town development in Europe and other parts of the world.

There was reluctance on our part to deal with new towns as an issue or an instrument for lower income housing, separate from the total housing problem throughout the country. By the same token there was a reluctance to deal with land policy in the very narrow category of new town development, rather than developing a national policy on national land use that was all-inclusive.

We finally came to the three points John (DeBoer) had asked us to consider. Some said they might possibly support a new town coalition although they would want to be certain there was no duplication. Others felt that their organizations might be interested in supporting such a coalition but could not at this time speak for their organizations.

Groups 3 and 4, FOSTER: I think Groups 3 and 4 meeting together would reiterate what Groups 1 and 2 said, especially the point that if there is to be another coalition it would have to have a very definitive role. Actually, four possibilities for coalitions were mentioned, and they are as follows: (1) a coalition with such tasks as reviewing project agreements and recommending additions to HUD regarding the Title VII program; (2) an advocate coalition for low or moderate income housing at the early stages of new community development; (3) a coalition to advocate and actually build low cost housing in new communities; and (4) a coalition to write legislation for new communities, adding additional legislation to that which already exists; this type of coalition would be a nob hill thing that would meet periodically.

We also raised this question: Would existing new communities like Reston or Columbia really accept low cost housing? Is this actually possible?

As the two previous groups stated, we should look at the existing coalitions and networks and see if we should not be joining them. We discussed the differences between networks and coalitions; it was the consensus of our group that the networks that get things done are informal and depend upon who knows who and who trusts who. Coalitions are more formalized and may not be as effective. We also discussed the role of the churches and how they might become involved in the land business itself in terms of buying up the land and giving it away to people who wanted to do their own thing. We thought such an approach on the part of the churches had possibilities.

The real question, we felt, was, "Can new towns provide housing for low income people?" We were not too hopeful about this because of the mores of our society and its economic structure. We did mention the business of jobs in relation to housing and saw this as a plus factor in new towns, since we place great value on the work ethic. But here, too, we weren't certain how this might work out in the long run.

Group 5, BROWN: Our group decided that we needed two more days just to deal with relating new towns to low income Americans. We began by talking about some of the things we felt were hinderances to housing low income Americans in new towns, with particular reference to the role of industry. Industry in new towns generally caters to the white collar worker and to middle and upper management. Also, most industries locating in new towns are environmentally clean, and clean industries generally have more skilled, rather than semi-skilled or unskilled, workers. If this latter group were to live in new towns it would have to find work elsewhere.

We also felt frustrated because the conference is so designed that the only answer you could make to the question, "Is there a need for a network of organizations to address the issue of the needs of lower income Americans in new towns?"—is Yes! But with all the differences expressed here today, and the limited time in which we had to grapple with this, we were at a loss to determine who should form this network, how many should be involved, and what their role or roles might be.

We recognized that the New Communities Act is good, but that it is without the resources for proper implementation. Further, there is no money in this Act for social, economic, or health planning. We felt there was a need to constitutionally establish the rights of the poor to adequate housing. If this could be established, provisions for land use would follow. It would also give initiative to the affirmative-action clause.

We recognized that most middle Americans react negatively to new towns, particularly as they relate to low income housing. Middle Americans also object to someone doing their planning for them and then telling them what to do.

We also discussed whether communities themselves could own new towns. At this stage of development this is theoretical, of course, but it's worth exploring in terms of land ownership and leasing. Such ownership might reduce cost by as much as 27 percent, and this is certainly something to consider.

We suggest that the Interreligious New Communities Coalition make available to all of the groups represented here the names of the coalitions that are already in existence to help these coalitions be supportive of one another. In that way we would all become aware of our mutual concerns, and all of us could better establish priorities.

DeBOER: I have been making notes and trying to sort out the underlying comments and themes. Before I do this, however, does anyone wish to add anything to any of the reports we've just listened to? Mr. Claytor, I believe you have an addendum for Group 5, and if there are any others who want to add to your report, which you would like for the record, please feel free to do so.

CLAYTOR: Just to amplify a remark made by the presenter. There are two items that I think should be noted. The first is that there seems to be a consensus that it was unfair to lay the problem of low income housing on new communities since it is a problem endemic to all communities, not just to new ones, and that if we impose low income housing on new towns we are forcing upon them an additional burden that might be totally impractical.

Second, we didn't quite say we wanted churches to give away their land. I think what we recommended was that a private land banking phenomenon not too dissimilar from the Hartford process, which is private and not governmental, be brought into the picture. That's something to shoot for, and then private groups such as churches and the like could do a little less talking and moralizing, and play more of an activist role by parting with some of the land they own. That might also take the form of acquiring land at market value and making it available to socially motivated groups that have the same interest as do the churches.

DeBOER: Are there any other additions anyone would like to make?

McKISSICK: There are two areas with which we should concern ourselves, and I don't think a good group like this one should just break up and go home without some objectives in mind to follow up. I would like to make two suggestions for the churches. The first is that churches involve themselves in free-standing new communities by actually creating free-standing new communities. By doing that they can relate to all the problems expressed today. Furthermore, the churches have the resources to do it. They can do the social planning without the government doing it for them. Secondly, there is no reason why the churches could not initiate new programs. A legislative committee could be created to frame legislation to be passed on or worked on in cooperation with other agencies, and certainly to champion the constitutional right of the poor to adequate housing. These are two of my suggestions, which will hopefully keep you from breaking up and going home without a demand made upon you.

WIREMAN: I want to add to that demand a request in terms of my staff responsibility at HUD. We at HUD are very grateful to be invited to a group such as this that has commitment, concern, interest, and expertise. I would urge that as much as possible you try and determine how to get the expertise that exists in this room about existing programs in new communities or old, circulated as quickly as possible. We should begin to more quickly share information with each other and with the League of New Community Developers and the developers of communities in your area. If you know of things that work, for heavens sake either share them at conferences or publish them so that they can be made available. I think a lot of understanding of how you actually do the nitty-gritties of a variety of social endeavors, from integrating a particular housing project to running a day-care center, unfortunately resides in individual heads and isn't shared. If you know of good things in this regard, please send them to me at HUD.

CONFEREE: How about the things that don't work?

WIREMAN: We should share those experiences, too, of course. Sometimes you learn more from things that don't work than from those that do.

DeBOER: While you're at the microphone, Ms. Wireman, may I ask if you know of any coalitions or networks that gather around the kinds of things we have been talking about today? There is the League of New Community Developers, I know. Are there other groups?

WIREMAN: Well, there is soon going to be an association of people who are concerned with social planning. As a matter of fact, it is having its first organizational meeting this evening in Columbia, Maryland.

DeBOER: Is this group specifically new town oriented?

WIREMAN: Yes. It is made up of people who are involved in social planning for new communities.

DeBOER: Anyone else?

JOHNSON: I just want to add that we should be aware of the national human priorities group that Barbara Williams directs, The Coalition For Human Needs at 1717 Massachusetts Avenue, Washington, D.C. We should feed into her organization the human priorities that we're thinking and talking about in reference to new communities.

There should be information-sharing that encompasses urban, suburban, exurban, rural, and new communities. That is the national human priorities agenda.

WIREMAN: I would like to make one further request. Several publications have recently raised the very serious question of whether it is possible to achieve both racial and class integration at once, and have stated that this has not been successfully accomplished in this country. Now, I happen to know of several places where it has been accomplished because I've lived in them. It would be useful to begin to accumulate a listing of places where people are in fact successfully integrated, either racially, by class, or both. We should be able to single out people who have some real expertise in this area and who can point to the things that must be done for such integration to work. This would be exceedingly useful to a developer.

DeBOER: Let me now try to summarize these group reports.

There is a strong thread of hesitancy running through all the groups about forming a coalition if coalitions dealing with our agenda already exist. The groups wanted to make certain there would be no duplication.

I think that is a valid concern. But in my running around, in my trying to determine what networks might exist addressing themselves to my question, "Are New Towns For Lower Income Americans Too?" I didn't find any. There is a new social planning organization that's developing and that was mentioned before. However, this meeting was called because there doesn't appear to be any other network addressed to our question.

The item of citizen participation surfaced in such questions as whether new towns should be community owned and whether they should be related to the people that are involved.

Also raised was the interrelationship of the various parts of the system: the relationship of the new town to the old town; the entire approach to housing; and the social planning aspects.

Discussed too was the need for legislative coordination. If there are to be some initiatives here, colleagues in this effort should be identified in order to take advantage of whatever expertise we have separately and that bear on the particular initiatives that are undertaken.

The possible role of religious groups as developers was raised. This is a concern that INCC has had theoretically on its agenda. However, things don't work any faster in the world of the church than anywhere else.

There is a need to identify hinderances to the more abundant life for everyone in new towns or old towns, to catalog and draw up the agenda for persons who want to work against these hinderances.

Regarding our basic question, the feeling I pick up from the various groups is, "A coalition? Well, maybe. We haven't had enough time to think about that. We certainly would want to think about it some more. We would want to know what that would involve". So there is a kind of a qualified yes or a "We're not sure." When it comes down to networks, I believe the feeling on that was quite positive. There were several people, including Peggy Wireman, who felt the need for a clearinghouse. We need to know what's going on. Somehow we need to be able to pick each other's brains. Someone asked, "Where's that list that you referred to? I'd like to get that list of new towns that INCC has been working at." Is this about where it's at? Maybe we don't know what is meant by a coalition. But a network, yes.

GREENDALE: As your Cochairman, I would just like to comment on coalitions. I am not aware of any coalitions that really direct themselves to our Conference theme. I attended the social planners' first meeting in Washington, and I, myself, raised this theme with them. But I don't think they address themselves to it, at least not yet. I don't know whether the National Committee Against Discrimination In Housing (Ed Holmgren, its director, is here) is addressing itself to this theme in relation to new towns.

I've studied this field since we at the American Jewish Committee formed our National Job-Linked-Housing Center, and I am not aware of any group that's relating to our theme as we have outlined it today. And may I add that we are subscribing to an advocacy role; we are saying that new towns in America as presently constituted are not for lower income Americans; and we are saying further that there must be a coalition to advocate inclusion of lower income Americans in new towns, and that this coalition should help the nation find the strategies and programs to make this possible.

CONFEREE: I, too, attended the first social planners' conference on new towns. I believe the theme that we have discussed today is being addressed by other groups, but perhaps the wrong way, and I think it's up to this group to try to redefine their direction to bring us all out at the same point. It's important for us to ask ourselves why other groups who are in a position to influence our concerns are not looking at this problem the way we are.

HOLMGREN: Reference has been made to the National Committee Against Discrimination in Housing. I want to describe precisely what we are doing, which has, I think, some relevance to this issue. We are concerned with providing low and moderate income housing in new communities, but only as part of a larger program that seems to me more important, the whole question of planning for housing allocations, including fair share plans. We have a major program right now that is planning to work with regional planning groups throughout the country, through the National Association of Regional Councils as well as a variety of other organizations, to promote the idea of planning for fair share allocations. Dayton, Ohio, is a model, but only one of the earlier such models. Several others are now being developed in various parts of the country.

My concern, as expressed in the buzz session, was that we're dealing with this problem too narrowly. If a coalition concerns itself only with the problem of providing low and moderate income housing in new communities, then as observed earlier by Cushing Dolbeare, it deals only with a very small portion of the total housing production that's going to be taking place over the next several years. I think we have to broaden the concept of the coalition and state its objectives in much larger terms.

DeBOER: Well, friends, I think we've come to the conclusion of the program. You may be interested to know that tomorrow, all day, the Interreligious New Communities Coalition will be meeting, and a very important item on its agenda is the output of what happened today. We have therefore been listening closely to what has been said, and if there are ways in which we feel we can begin to implement some of the things that surfaced here, we will probably do so. We will be free to participate as the spirit moves or as the time makes clear. Thank you very much for being a part of this, and "God bless us everyone."

ABOUT THE EDITORS

JOHN C. DeBOER, Secretary for New Church Development and New Towns, United Church of Christ, was born in Kodiakinal, India. He went to elementary and high school in India and finished his final high school year at the Collegiate School in New York City. He has a B.S. in aeronautical engineering from the University of Michigan, a B.D. from the New Brunswick Theological Seminary, and an M.A. in urban sociology from Drew University. Prior to his becoming affiliated with the Church he was an aeronautical engineer with Convair in San Diego and Grauman on Long Island.

He has written extensively on new towns and spent 1972 in Europe, America, and Japan doing a study on the relationship of organized religion to new towns. He is a former chairman of the Interreligious New Communities Coalition and the current chairman of the Church Development Task Force of the Joint Strategy and Action Committee. He has published extensively and has contributed to the following periodicals: Church Management, Advance, United Church Herald, New World Outlook, and Ministers Quarterly. His published books include Let's Plan: A Guide to the Planning Process for Voluntary Organizations, Pilgrim Press, 1970; How to Succeed in the Organizational Jungle without Losing Your Religion, Pilgrim Press, 1972; and is currently at work on New Towns and Organized Religion.

ALEXANDER GREENDALE, National Director of the American Jewish Committee's Housing Division and its National Job-Linked-Housing Center, shares in the responsibility of developing and implementing the American Jewish Committee program in metropolitan areas. His major concentration is on intergroup relations as they affect housing. He is also responsible for providing guidelines and assistance to local AJC Chapters in their work in this field.

A trained social worker with a B.A. from the University of Hawaii, an M.A. from Stanford University, and an M.S.S. from Adelphi University, Mr. Greendale has had extensive experience in working with low and moderate and middle income families. Prior to joining AJC's National Staff he was project specialist with the Community Service Society of New York, in which he directed a family life education and management training demonstration program sponsored jointly with the New York City Housing Authority. In the 1960s he was director of the Department of Community Work and Housing for the Lenox Hill Neighborhood Association. He has been a lecturer at the City College of New York, Barnard College, and the Adelphi

University School of Social Work. He is the current chairman of the Interreligious New Communities Coalition and is a member of the National Association of Housing and Redevelopment Officials and the National Association of Social Workers.

He has published The Kipling Sampler, Fawcett Publications, 1945, second edition, 1947; Life in Public Housing Equals Tenants plus Management, Community Service Society of New York, 1971; Guidelines to Scatter Site Public Housing, American Jewish Committee, 1971; and Jobs and the Missing Link—Housing, The National Job-Linked-Housing Center, 1972.

Before going into social work, Mr. Greendale was a dramatist. He had numerous productions, among them "Walk Into My Parlor" produced on Broadway in 1941. He was the recipient of many major playwriting fellowships and awards, including the Rockefeller, Theater Guild, and Guggenheim Fellowships, and awards from the American Academy of Arts and Letters and the American National Theater and Academy.

RELATED TITLES
Published by
Praeger Special Studies

NEW TOWNS: WHY—AND FOR WHOM?
     edited by
     Harvey S. Perloff
     and Neil C. Sandberg

NEW TOWNS AND COMMUNAL VALUES:
Case Study of Columbia, Maryland
     Richard Oliver Brooks

FINANCIAL ANALYSIS AND THE NEW
COMMUNITY DEVELOPMENT PROCESS
     Richard L. Heroux
     and William A. Wallace

EXCLUSIONARY ZONING: Land Use Regulation
and Housing in the 1970s
     Richard F. Babcock
     and Fred P. Bosselman